Cambridge Elements ≡

Elements in Criminology
edited by
David Weisburd
George Mason University, Virginia
Hebrew University of Jerusalem

MAKING SENSE OF YOUTH CRIME

A Comparison of Police Intelligence in the United States and France

Jacqueline E. Ross
University of Illinois College of Law
Thierry Delpeuch
CNRS and Grenoble Alpes University

CAMBRIDGE
UNIVERSITY PRESS

CAMBRIDGE
UNIVERSITY PRESS

Shaftesbury Road, Cambridge CB2 8EA, United Kingdom

One Liberty Plaza, 20th Floor, New York, NY 10006, USA

477 Williamstown Road, Port Melbourne, VIC 3207, Australia

314–321, 3rd Floor, Plot 3, Splendor Forum, Jasola District Centre, New Delhi – 110025, India

103 Penang Road, #05–06/07, Visioncrest Commercial, Singapore 238467

Cambridge University Press is part of Cambridge University Press & Assessment, a department of the University of Cambridge.

We share the University's mission to contribute to society through the pursuit of education, learning and research at the highest international levels of excellence.

www.cambridge.org
Information on this title: www.cambridge.org/9781009364287

DOI: 10.1017/9781009364263

First published 2023

A catalogue record for this publication is available from the British Library.

ISBN 978-1-009-36428-7 Paperback
ISSN 2633-3341 (online)
ISSN 2633-3333 (print)

Making Sense of Youth Crime

A Comparison of Police Intelligence in the United States and France

Elements in Criminology

DOI: 10.1017/9781009364263
First published online: February 2023

Jacqueline E. Ross
University of Illinois College of Law

Thierry Delpeuch
CNRS and Grenoble Alpes University

Author for correspondence: Jacqueline E. Ross, jeross1@illinois.edu

Abstract: This comparative empirical study of policing in the United States and France draws on the authors' ten years of field work to contend that the police in both countries should be thought about as an amalgam of five distinct professional cultures or "intelligence regimes" – each of which can be found in any given police department in both the United States and France. In particular, it is contended that what police do as knowledge workers and how they make sense of the social problems such as collective offending by juveniles varies with the professional subcommunities or "intelligence regimes" in which their particular knowledge work is embedded. The same problem can be looked at in fundamentally different ways even within a single police department, depending on the intelligence regime through which the problem is refracted.

Keywords: policing, intelligence, analysts, gangs, juveniles

ISBNs: 9781009364287 (PB), 9781009364263 (OC)
ISSNs: 2633-3341 (online), 2633-3333 (print)

Contents

1 Introduction

Improving the ways in which the police make sense of crime is the subject of a growing body of literature that seeks to reform and expand the role of intelligence analysis within the police. Addressing crime more effectively, scholars contend, requires outside expertise in intelligence-led policing, evidence-based policing, hot spot policing, and problem-solving policing, to name only a few of the most notable police reform initiatives.[1] What reformers currently fail to consider, however, is how their proposed improvements mesh (or fail to mesh) with the knowledge work the police are already performing. Nor do existing reform proposals recognize let alone differentiate between the *multiplicity* of knowledge communities within the police – a necessary task if reformers want to tailor their preferred analytical approach to the knowledge community that is most likely to be both suitable and receptive.

This comparative empirical study of policing in the United States and France draws on the authors' ten years of field work (2007 to 2017, see Section 2) to contend that the police in both countries should be thought about as an amalgam of five distinct professional cultures or "intelligence regimes" – each of which can be found in any given police department in both the United States and France. Each of these intelligence regimes, we contend, has its own characteristic interpretive frameworks, time horizons, and ecology of actors, and each feed into different modes of police intervention. Nor is all of this analytical work performed by something called an "intelligence unit"; we found that discrete pockets of dedicated expertise, with their own analytical traditions and tools, can be found at all levels of the police hierarchy, from top leadership, middle management, to detectives investigating crime; partnership liaison officers who deliberate with community stakeholders and residents; and street cops responding to calls for service.

---

[1] J. Ratcliffe (2016), *Intelligence-Led Policing*, 2nd ed., London: Routledge; J. G. Carter (2013), *Intelligence-Led Policing: A Policing Innovation*, El Paso, TX: LFB Scholarly Publishing; D. Weisburd & A. A. Braga, eds. (2006), *Police Innovation: Contrasting Perspectives*, Cambridge: Cambridge University Press; H. Goldstein (1990), *Problem-Oriented Policing*, New York: McGraw-Hill; A. Braga (2010), *Problem-Oriented Policing & Crime Prevention*, 2nd ed., Boulder, CO: Lynne Rienner; K. Bullock, R. Erol, & N. Tilley (2006), *Problem-Oriented Policing and Partnerships: Implementing an Evidence-Based Approach to Crime Reduction*, Portland, OR: Willan; J. Ratcliffe (2019), *Reducing Crime: A Companion for Police Leaders*, Oxon: Routledge; D. H. Bayley (1994), *Police for the Future*, Oxford: Oxford University Press; D. H. Bayley & P. C. Stenning (2016), *Governing the Police: Experience in Six Democracies*, New Brunswick, NJ: Transaction; D. Weisburd, J. E. Eck, A. A. Braga et al. (2016), *Place Matters: Criminology for the Twenty-First Century*, Cambridge: Cambridge University Press; D. Wisler & I. D. Onwudiwe, eds. (2009), *Community Policing: International Patterns and Comparative Perspectives*, Boca Raton, FL: CRC Press.

Haggerty and Ericsson have famously characterized police as knowledge workers.[2] Peter Manning, too, urges readers to "consider the police organization as a context for information processing."[3] But Manning notes that "[t]here are few studies of police management or top command and their work."[4] Studies of police as knowledge workers are limited by focusing mainly on street-level actors, particularly patrol, perhaps because studies of patrol lend themselves to ride-alongs that reveal the day-to-day work environment of frontline officers and first responders.[5] Through field work with middle and upper management as well as frontline officers in both the United States and France, we compared the ways in which distinct pockets within the police of both countries interpret the collective criminal activity of young people, whether gang-related or not. To what extent do different professional subcommunities within the police view membership in a youth gang as useful in explaining collective criminal offending by young people? What difference, we wanted to know, does the institutional vantage point make to the way in which the police explain violence and other collective action by young people? We contend that what police do as knowledge workers and how they make sense of the social problems they are asked to address varies with the professional subcommunities or "intelligence regimes" in which their particular knowledge work is embedded.

Collective juvenile offending, we contend, is particularly apt to look different from multiple vantage points because it brings under one umbrella so many different phenomena whose connections with each other and with gang activity are contested, from loitering, vandalism, and open-air drug trafficking, to aggravated assault and homicide. We focus specifically on *collective* juvenile offending because "adolescent crimes ... are committed predominantly by groups, not by offenders acting alone."[6]

Though we deal, in part, with the ways in which police make sense of gangs, we speak of "collective juvenile offending" more generally, as the decision to apply this term to a group of juveniles who are "loitering," selling drugs, or engaging in violence is itself a part of what we are studying. When do the police in each country find it useful to interpret problem behaviors by groups of young people as gang-related, and what alternative constructions are available to them in their professional routines?

---

[2] R. H. Ericson & K. Haggerty (1997), *Policing the Risk Society*, Toronto: University of Toronto Press.

[3] P. K. Manning (2018), Technology, Law, and Policing, in M. den Boer, ed., *Comparative Policing from a Legal Perspective*, Cheltenham: Edward Elgar, 290–305, 291.

[4] *Ibid.*, 303.   [5] *Ibid.*, 303.

[6] D. A. Sklansky (2021), *A Pattern of Violence: How the Law Classifies Crimes and What it Means for Justice*, Cambridge, MA: The Belknap Press, 174.

Our answers to these questions emerge out of a comparison of two very different policing systems which "form a kind of commentary on one another's character."[7] An "individuating comparison" makes visible features of contrasting systems that might otherwise escape notice. In this case, the juxtaposition of the United States and France reveals deep structural similarities that transcend differences between the underlying criminal phenomena and between law enforcement institutions. Cross-national comparisons across extremely different policing institutions help bring out the defining characteristics of distinct intelligence regimes precisely because, as our research suggests, policing systems as different from each other as those of the United States and France display the same pattern. Indeed, our research reveals striking cross-national affinities between the ways in which the cities of Chicago and Marseille address retaliatory violence by drug trafficking organizations by young people, even though these problems are not considered gang-related in Marseille, as they are in Chicago. Both cities mobilize the same intelligence regime as the primary interpretive lenses for dealing with retaliatory shootings. Similar affinities exist between the approaches of Nantes, in France, and Aurora, Illinois, suggesting the difference the choice of intelligence regime makes to the way in which police from very different legal systems address a given problem.

Section 2 describes our research methodology. Section 3 introduces the concept of an "intelligence regime" and its value to understanding the knowledge work of law enforcement agencies in making sense of a complex phenomenon like that of collective juvenile offending. Section 4 sets out and illustrates the five intelligence regimes with examples from our field work, arguing that these five professional subcultures structure the knowledge work of police in both the United States and France, despite the profound systemic differences between the policing institutions of the two countries. Section 5 explores tensions between distinct intelligence regimes, while Section 6 contends that intelligence regimes mediate and shape intelligence-led approaches to crime and that any given police approach to collective juvenile offending must be designed to further synergies and reduce tensions between distinct intelligence regimes, while matching any given reform initiative with the intelligence regime that has the greatest affinity for its outlook and methods. Section 7 concludes that a city's approach to the problem of collective youth crime reflects a deeply pragmatic choice between multiple competing analytical frameworks and can best be understood as a function of which intelligence regimes have been chosen to take the lead in addressing the problem, and of how the dominant regime has been coordinated with the others.

---

[7] C. J. Geertz (1968), *Islam Observed*, Chicago, IL: University of Chicago Press, 4.

2 Our Methodology

We propose a framework for distinguishing between what we term "intelligence regimes" within the police, drawing on our own empirical research into French and American policing, from 2007 to 2017. We will draw on our research (a) in presenting our framework for differentiating among intelligence communities and (b) in describing how these distinct professional cultures shape a range of distinct ways in which the police think about collective juvenile delinquency.[8]

Many different forms of police expertise touch on some aspect of juvenile collective offending. Our qualitative interviews and observational data were designed to generate rather than test theories about how distinct knowledge communities within the police are organized to acquire, analyze, and use intelligence about their respective areas of expertise – and how their distinctive characteristics compare with each other.[9] Our research encompassed ride-alongs with ground-level actors and 500 semistructured, open-ended qualitative interviews with a wide range of knowledge workers within the police, including understudied policing actors such as intelligence analysts, partnership liaisons, as well as middle managers and chiefs of the command hierarchy. We combined the "informal conversational interview" with elements of the "general interview guide approach," in which the investigator uses a checklist of issues to be explored but adapts the wording and order of questions to the expertise of individual respondents.[10]

Our research sites spanned multiple cities in the United States and France, and we illustrate our regimes with interview data and observational data drawn from Marseille, St. Etienne, Cenon, Nantes, Vitry-le-Francois, and Grenoble, in France, and from Aurora, Illinois and Chicago, in the United States. In each country, we chose sites that had tried out a variety of different approaches to persistent crime problems, and we attempted to include both smaller and larger cities in diverse geographical regions of each country. We spent between two and six weeks at each location, usually in one-week stints over the course of several months. Most individual interviews lasted from two to three hours, with some lasting much longer, and we frequently reinterviewed members of the

---

[8] All interviews are on file with the authors.

[9] R. Swedberg (2012), Theorizing in Sociology and Social Science: Turning to the Context of Discovery, *Theory and Society* 41:1–40; D. Rueschemeyer (2009), *Usable Theory: Analytic Tools for Social and Political Research*, Princeton, NJ: Princeton University Press.

[10] See M. Q. Patton (2014), *Qualitative Evaluation and Research Methods*, 4th ed., Newbury Park, CA: Sage; Y. S. Lincoln & E. G. Guba (1985), *Naturalistic Inquiry*, Newbury Park, CA: Sage; I. Seidman (1998), *Interviewing as Qualitative Research*, 2nd ed., New York: Teachers' College Press; G. King, R. O. Keohane, & S. Verba (1994), *Designing Social Inquiry: Scientific Inference in Qualitative Research*, Princeton, NJ: Princeton University Press; J. Maanen, ed. (1998), *Qualitative Studies of Organizations*, Thousand Oaks, CA: Sage.

command hierarchy over the course of our stay at each location. At each site we interviewed the command hierarchy, seeking out supervisors, community policing specialists, and partnership liaisons who relied on intelligence to solve particular crime problems or to address the demands of local stakeholders, and we collected examples of the intelligence products on which they relied. Our interlocutors did not come only from units expressly denominated as intelligence units, though we met with analysts and supervisors from every type of intelligence unit present in each location, along with supervisors at fusion centers in the United States and their counterparts in the Renseignements Territoriaux; the Direction Generale de Securite Interieure; the intelligence cells of the Gendarmerie; the SIRASCO (criminal intelligence units in the National Police); and the SIRASCO's counterparts in the Gendarmerie. We also interviewed local stakeholders (such as prosecutors, municipal officials, political leaders, housing, transportation and school officials, social workers, and a variety of nongovernmental organizations) who played a role in partnership deliberations and problem-solving.

We used our interview and observational data to search for patterns along the dimensions of analysis (time horizons, aims, tools, criteria of validity, etc.). In particular, we focused on the ways in which knowledge workers doing very different kinds of police work collected, analyzed, and used information, and on the ways in which intelligence fed into the decision-making processes of the ecology of actors who generated, evaluated, and used it. We derived our intelligence regimes inductively, through the data we draw on below (a) to illustrate the various categories that make up the regime and (b) to illustrate our cross-national comparison.

3 On the Notion of an Intelligence Regime

Even within the same police department, we contend, intelligence regimes offer distinct perspectives on the complex phenomena that make up "collective juvenile offending." And each regime may help remedy the blind spots of another. David Sklansky contends, for example, that "the criminal law ... has come to reflect a view of violence as characterological rather than situational,"[11] but one reason why the social and situational context of juvenile delinquency may be ignored by prosecutors and detectives is that this is not what criminal investigation is set up to address. If "criminal law has a long tradition of treating groups of offenders acting together as especially threatening and warranting special sanctions,"[12] other intelligence regimes that are not institutionally invested in building cases for criminal prosecution may be more willing to entertain Sklansky's "doubt whether many

---

[11] Sklansky, *A Pattern of Violence*, 8.   [12] *Ibid.*, 163.

gangs were as organized or as powerful as law enforcement . . . made them out to be."[13] Other institutional actors may be more attentive to contextual factors, including situational triggers, neighborhood characteristics, group dynamics, and opportunity structures (for education, mentoring, recreation, and employment) that make young people vulnerable to recruitment by gangs.

The intelligence regimes we introduce thus capture the differences between five ways of thinking about a problem like collective juvenile disorder in the public realm, whether designated as gang-related or not. Viewed as a crime problem, these phenomena might yield prosecutions of offender groups as racketeering enterprises (in the United States) or as manifestations of organized crime (in France). Viewed as public safety problems, through the lens of social contagion, the same problems might produce efforts to anticipate, predict, de-escalate, and head off future incidents. As an order maintenance problem, collective juvenile offending might be treated as a neighborhood-specific quality of life issue requiring ground-level actors to get to know local schools, local kids, and local hangouts. As a challenge for local security partnerships, collective juvenile offending may invite participants to focus on poorly designed common areas, limited summer jobs, the needs of under-served age groups, and the lack of recreational spaces. And if treated as an occasion for managerial oversight over enforcement strategy, analysis might focus on concerns about the effectiveness of stop-and-frisk strategies and their alienating impact on communities of color, or about the ways in which racketeering prosecutions of large street gangs have fragmented fairly stable street gangs into smaller, more volatile rivals for contested terrain. What sets these regimes apart from each other is the kind of information they value; the ecology of actors who participate in a particular regime; the ways in which members of each regime process and analyze information; the tools and frameworks they use for that purpose; and the ways in which they use the information to guide official action.

We challenge monist generalizations about the professional culture of the police that view the police as generally suspicious of new intelligence techniques[14] or as generally hostile to outsiders.[15] There is no such thing as a monolithic "police culture," we contend, though some scholars, like Jerome Skolnick, at times speak of typical ways in which police perceive and interpret the world around them.[16] Skolnick, Waddington, and Van Maanen build their

---

[13] *Ibid.*

[14] J. B. Chan (1997), *Changing Police Culture: Policing in a Multicultural Society*, Cambridge: Cambridge University Press.

[15] R. Reiner (2000), *The Politics of the Police*, Oxford: Oxford University Press.

[16] J. H. Skolnick (1994), *Justice without Trial: Law Enforcement in a Democratic Society*, 3rd ed., New York: Wiley.

description of the police world and its characteristic outlook around the tendency of many police officers to foreground their crime-fighting functions, even though this is, for most officers, only a small part of what they do.[17] Reiner and Crank in turn speak of an us-against-them mentality toward the poor and toward racial and ethnic minorities.[18] Westley and Jerome Hall, too, viewed the police as a cohesive occupational group acculturated to a shared set of norms,[19] without taking account of the variability of assignments and roles within the police. However, in both the United States and in France, most studies of policing to make these claims have focused on ground-level operational units. With less attention paid to the distinctive tool kits and institutional interests of intelligence analysts, local security partnerships, middle management, or the general staff, it becomes difficult to appreciate the plurality of professional cultures within the police and to determine how differences between professional cultures translate into distinct approaches to problems such as gang crime and other forms of collective offending by young people.

James Q. Wilson, for example, theorized important differences in policing "styles" by distinguishing among the norms and practices peculiar to the *watchman* style (with its characteristic concern with suppression of the visible signs of social disorders), the *service* style (with its emphasis on responding to community complaints and deliberating with outsiders about how to handle local concerns), and the *legalistic* style (with its focus on crime fighting and legal outputs in the form of criminal prosecutions).[20] But he confined these observations to ground-level personnel in what we would term the order maintenance regime and attributed the style the at each location to the police organization as a whole, without considering the possibility that multiple "styles" might inhere and coexist in distinct professional subcultures under the umbrella of one institution.

In lieu of policing "styles" that accrue to police departments as a whole, we posit multiple professional cultures that guide the ways in which the police evaluate situations, select a course of action, and justify their actions to other members of the organization.[21] As early as 1983, in the English-speaking

---

[17] *Ibid*; J. Van Maanen (1978), The Asshole, in P. K. Manning & J. Van Maanen, eds., *Policing: A View from the Street*, Santa Monica, CA: Goodyear, 221–237; P. A. J. Waddington (1999), Police (Canteen) Sub-culture: An Appreciation, *British Journal of Criminology* 39(2):287–309.

[18] Reiner, *The Politics of the Police*; J. P. Crank (1994), Watchman and Community: Myth and Institutionalization in Policing, *Law & Society Review* 28(2):325–352.

[19] J. Hall (1953), Police and Law in a Democratic Society, *Indiana Law Journal* 28:133–177; W. Westley (1953), Violence and the Police: A Sociological Study of Law, Custom, and Morality, *American Journal of Sociology* 59:34–41.

[20] J. Q. Wilson (1968), *Varieties of Police Behavior*, Cambridge, MA: Harvard University Press.

[21] Chan, *Changing Police Culture*; E. A. Paoline (2003), Taking Stock: Towards a Richer Understanding of Police Culture, *Journal of Criminal Justice* 31(3):199–214.

literature, Elizabeth Reuss-Ianni focused on differences between the police cultures of *street cops* and *management cops*, attributing the gulf between them to the increasing desire of the command hierarchy to demonstrate the efficiency and productivity of their work force. Peter Manning in turn differentiates the outlooks and professional cultures of patrol units, first responders (with largely reactive responsibilities), and proactive drug investigators.[22]

But while Manning recognizes that "police occupational culture is multifaceted,"[23] he distinguishes between parts of the police apparatus based on activities (like patrol), specialized expertise (detectives, special units), and place in the top-down command hierarchy (middle management, top command), while our ideal-typical intelligence regimes focus on the ecosystem – the knowledge environment – in which officers are embedded. Our evidence suggests that officers from different units or different levels of the command hierarchy may share the same aims, outlook, analytical frameworks, and time horizons with each other when they seek to predict and to forestall retaliatory gang violence, riots, or protests, while two detectives in the same division may belong to different intelligence regimes and function very differently from each other, if one of them is assigned to helping a task force build racketeering cases against gang leaders for past offenses, making the officer part of the criminal intelligence regime, while the other arrests a gang member for a probation violation or technical weapons infraction to stave off retaliatory violence in the immediate aftermath of a gang-related shooting, which in turn makes that officer part of the public safety regime, with its focus on anticipating future "outbreaks" of violence on an "epidemiological" model of gang violence.

In France, Dominique Monjardet, whose work inspired our own typology, differentiated among professional *attitudes* and *modes of production* rather than *styles*,[24] categorizing three modes of police work as public safety, order maintenance, and the building of criminal cases, though partnership and managerial decision-making did not figure in the mix. But while Monjardet's typology focuses primarily on police work, rather than the diverse cognitive frameworks that support these activities and make them meaningful to their protagonists, we have reconfigured our typology into ideal types of conceptually distinct knowledge communities each of which has its own ways of making sense of security problems, its own time horizons, its own ecology of actors, and its own professional routines.

---

[22] P. K. Manning (2008), *The Technology of Policing: Crime Mapping, Information Technology, and the Rationality of Crime Control*, New York: New York University Press.

[23] Manning, Technology, Law, and Policing, 302.

[24] D. Monjardet (1996), *Ce que fait la police*, Paris: La Découverte.

Monjardet links different types of policing activities closely to their institutional homes, i.e. to the units which perform them; however, we have found that individual units shift back and forth between these different types of activities and that expertise and know-how can migrate across units. Indeed, the same individual within any given unit may shift back and forth between intelligence regimes, depending on whether she is, say, helping detectives and prosecutors to interview a witness about a gang-related shooting that occurred a year earlier (criminal intelligence), dispatching police cars to respond to a gang fight in progress (order maintenance intelligence) or preparing a chart to track the average time emergency units took to respond to calls about gang fights in progress (managerial intelligence).

Fabien Jobard and Jacques de Maillard's account of police work[25] in turn differentiates between order maintenance, investigative policing, and policing of crowds.[26] But unlike Jobard and de Maillard, who treat information policing as a distinct police activity, we view the collection, analysis, and use of information as integral to all police activities and seek to differentiate the roles information plays across organizational contexts and tasks. Intelligence analysis, we contend, is not unique to intelligence units. Intelligence gathering plays a role in all police activities.[27] All knowledge communities within the police develop their own interpretive lenses and analytical tools. Within the police, there are multiple different ways of analyzing phenomena that serve the practical needs of each distinct knowledge community. What sets intelligence regimes apart, we contend, is the way in which their adherents seek out and make sense of information, and the uses for which they develop their analyses.

Accordingly, our ideal types juxtapose the purposes for which members of intelligence regimes pursue information, and the interpretive frameworks they privilege. Attention to the types of information each intelligence regime seeks out can in turn reveal fundamental differences between intelligence regimes that have affinities for open-source over closed-source intelligence; for secret over open exchanges; for bilateral exchanges with privileged sources over multilateral negotiated exchanges with institutional partners; or for observations assessed through situation sense and prior experience in lieu of intelligence

---

[25] F. Jobard & J. de Maillard (2015), *Sociologie de la Police*, Paris: Armand Colin.

[26] Sheptycki, too, differentiates between distinct "foci" of police intelligence work, though he, like Manning, sees most of these "foci" as deviations from the dominant *métier* of policing, to which case work and the search for evidence – what we term the criminal intelligence regime – remains central. J. Sheptycki (2017), The Police Intelligence Division of Labour, *Policing and Society* 27(6):620–635.

[27] Indeed, the claim of special expertise in intelligence matters is a mode of self-presentation and therefore no less subject to empirical scrutiny than the claim often made by members of the French National Gendarmerie that all of its officers are trained as intelligence captors.

that has been cross-checked, corroborated, and evaluated for its reliability; human intelligence over signals intelligence; and so forth.

In comparison with typologies that focus only on the activities of the police, the focus on professional cultures as cognitive communities can expose the symbiotic relationship between analytical frames and modes of intervention, that is, between ways of seeing and ways of acting. Different cognitive communities have distinctive intelligence tools and develop their own ways of aggregating information and of searching for patterns in the data they collect. For example, an intelligence unit that relies on predictive algorithms of repetitive criminal activity and has access to highly mobile rapid intervention teams may use data about shifting outbreaks of gang violence to implement saturation tactics (as Chicago's intelligence unit did in 2008–2010, in shifting from saturating the neighborhood where violence occurred to suturing the neighborhood where retaliatory violence is expected).

Understanding intelligence regimes is essential to implementing police reforms, we contend, because the impact of any given reform initiative is mediated by the intelligence regimes through which it is routed and implemented. One reason for this is that "the adoption of innovation is determined primarily by the experiences of practitioners and often has little to do with research evidence."[28] Reform strategies stand a better chance of success when they are matched with regimes whose practitioners have a natural affinity for the approach and tactics favored by a given reform strategy, that is, when they mesh with the outlook of participants in the intelligence regime that is given primary responsibility for implementing the initiative. Hot-spot policing, for example, which promotes the efficacy of "concentrating police in a few locations," depends heavily on crime mapping, which fits easily into the public safety and order maintenance regimes.[29] Already during the 1970s, Weisburd and Braga note, "crime analysts looked for patterns in crime by plotting the locations and times at which crimes were committed to direct patrol officers to the most likely targets."[30] Hot spots policing allows police to "continue to do what they do best – undercover and visible enforcement activities – but with greater efficiency and focus on specific locations."[31]

If the hot-spots approach meshes easily with order maintenance or public safety approaches to crime, which rely heavily on crime-mapping and directed

---

[28] D. Weisburd & A. A. Braga (2006), Hot Spots Policing as a Model for Police Innovation, in Weisburd & Braga, *Police Innovation*, 238.

[29] L. W. Sherman & D. Weisburd (1995), General Deterrent Effects of Police Patrol in Crime "Hot Spots": A Randomized Controlled Trial, *Justice Quarterly* 12:625–648.

[30] Weisburd & Braga, Hot Spots Policing, 236.

[31] D. P. Rosenbaum (2006), The Limits of Hot Spots Policing, in Weisburd & Braga, *Police Innovation*, 245.

patrols, the Boston Gun Project instead relied on the partnership regime to implement a problem-oriented approach to place-based gangs. Boston's initiative benefited from being embedded in local security partnerships, because this enabled the police to rely on the prestige and influence of local religious leaders to disrupt ongoing gang conflicts.[32]

Among reform initiatives, "community policing involves the most radical change to existing police orgs," because community policing looks to nonpolice actors as problem-solving partners, not simply as information sources.[33] This makes the partnership intelligence regime the natural home for community policing reforms. Participants in the partnership regime are less suspicious than the police rank and file of community policing because the partnership regime, like community policing, places heavy reliance on consultation with local stakeholders and de-escalation though nonpolice actors, including mediators, social workers, and violence interrupters in local communities.

By contrast, Compstat, which provides the command hierarchy with metadata on police performance,[34] supports managerial intelligence and the command hierarchy's quest for more efficient and effective use of police resources. In New York City, police leadership encouraged decentralized problem-solving and experimentation with new approaches by local commanders who operated within the order maintenance regime, as managerial decision-makers now possessed better tools for quantifying and evaluating the effectiveness of innovative approaches to a wide range of security concerns.[35]

Discrete reform proposals may speak to different intelligence regimes within the police and may be accommodated in the same policing apparatus when matched with distinct intelligence regimes that have an affinity for the reform proposal's methods and outlook. When reforms spearheaded by one intelligence regime fail, police may turn to a different intelligence regime for an entirely different paradigm. This is what happened in Chicago, we show, when racketeering prosecutions fragmented gangs and increased retaliatory violence. Chicago's shift to predictive algorithms as an alternative can be seen, we contend, as a wholesale shift from a criminal intelligence to a public safety approach to the problem. Exactly the opposite dynamic drove Marseille to shift to a criminal intelligence paradigm that treated open-air drug markets as a form of organized crime, after the perceived failure of its prior public safety approach

---

[32] *Ibid.*, 247.

[33] A. A. Braga & D. Weisburd (2006), Conclusion: Police Innovation and the Future of Policing, in Weisburd & Braga, *Police Innovation*, 346.

[34] E. B. Silverman (2006), Compstat's Innovation, in Weisburd & Braga, *Police Innovation*, 275.

[35] D. Weisburd, S. D. Mastrofski, J. J. Willis, & R. Greenspan (2006), Changing Everything So That Everything Can Remain the Same: Compstat and American Policing, in Weisburd & Braga, *Police Innovation*, 286.

to the problem. This shift in strategy is the purview of the managerial regime, which selects a dominant strategy and coordinates the other four regimes.

4 How Similarities between French and American Intelligence Regimes Transcend Institutional Differences

Despite the enormous structural differences between the fragmented American policing institutions and the highly centralized National Police and National Gendarmerie in France, we found, the same five intelligence regimes structured the collection and analysis of crime, and of collective juvenile offending, in particular, in both countries.

To be sure, as we show, national differences in approach to these problems are very real. In France, where policing initially developed as a response to threats to the state,[36] the police remain concerned, first and foremost, with riots and protests, often involving young people, which represent challenges to the authority of the state. By contrast, the primary problem of collective violence by young in the United States has become that of gang violence, which has historically been treated as a crime problem affecting the public, not as a form of protest against the state.[37] As a result, perhaps, of this ingrained difference between a police that grew up to protect the state and a police that developed to protect local communities, France has a national policing system,[38] split between a national police and a national gendarmerie, while the U.S. constitution, does not entrust policing to the federal government, in the first instance, yielding a decentralized and highly fragmented system of policing that is largely anchored in the needs and politics of local communities.

In France, we show, the multiple overlapping variants of collective offending by young people, mixing protests, riots, drug trafficking, soccer-related violence, and gang affiliation, make for a managerial intelligence system intent on disentangling disparate strands of collective activity by young people. In the US, gang affiliation was instead assumed to be the main driver of collective

---

[36] J. P. Brodeur (2010), *The Policing Web*, Oxford: Oxford University Press; M. Anderson (2011), *In Thrall to Political Change: Police and Gendarmerie in France*, Oxford: Oxford University Press.

[37] C. Emsley (1999), *Gendarmes and the State in Nineteenth Century Europe*, Oxford: Oxford University Press, 2.

[38] "Most of the nineteenth century and the first half of the twentieth century can be characterized by the efforts of central governments [in France] to reassert control over the police while legally maintain the fiction of some form of local responsibility." B. Dupont (2008), The French Police System: Caught between a Rock and a Hard Place – The Tension of Serving Both the State and the Public, in M. R. Haberfeld & I. Cerrah, eds., *Comparative Policing: The Struggle for Democratization*. Thousand Oaks, CA: Sage, 247–276. Dupont describes the French policing as "probably one of the most centralized administrative systems in the world, particularly in terms of policing." *Ibid.*, 256.

juvenile offending involving drugs or violence. As a result, the United States has proven far more willing than France to cast gangs as racketeering enterprises and to charge them with violations of statutes initially designed for organized crime. In France, gangs themselves are rarely treated as criminal organizations, and French initiatives against rioting groups of juveniles, local drug traffickers, and soccer fan clubs rarely try to break up the organizations themselves but focus instead on disrupting and abating their resort to violence.

Both France and the United States use local security partnerships to analyze clusters of collaborative juvenile offending at the neighborhood level. But in France, local security partnerships also differed from their American counterparts by not being embedded in a community policing paradigm. In the United States, partnerships were introduced as part of the community policing movement, which sought to improve day-to-day contacts between police and the neighborhoods they patrolled, while emphasizing the provision of public services as a key police role.[39] In France, where then Interior Minister Sarkozy rejected community policing in 2003 and where it was never fully revived, partnerships compensate to some extent for the lack of contact with local communities, and for the consequent loss of intelligence that accompanied the end of community policing.[40] American beat meetings bring police together with local residents, while French partnerships connect the police with other institutional stakeholders from education, social work, housing, and public transport, who act as intermediaries and replay or interpret the concerns of local residents. And because they serve local, not national authorities, American police are better positioned than their French counterparts to broker their connections with other city departments and to present themselves as able to help residents get graffiti removed and repairs made.[41]

There are other significant differences between the ways local security partnerships in the US and France approach collective juvenile disorder. As a result of the assumption that complex forms of collective disorder include both criminal and noncriminal strands, nonpolice participants in some French partnerships have been able to take a leading role in defining security problems and trying out new approaches, by comparison with their American counterparts. We show that in Nantes, for example, the mayor's office conducts its own fine-grained investigations and analysis of youth loitering complaints, to determine whether what is sometimes described as "juvenile take-over of public spaces"

---

[39] W. G. Skogan (2006), The Promise of Community Policing, in Weisburd & Braga, *Police Innovation*, 27.

[40] T. Delpeuch & J. E. Ross (Spring 2017), The Co-production of Security: A Comparative Study of the United States and France, *American Journal of Criminal Law* 44:117, 187–216.

[41] *Ibid.*

involves students who lack recreational spaces or gang members, and whether these young people who are using the location live nearby or have appropriated the space for open-air drug markets.

When the criminal nature of gang activity is presupposed, as in the US, it is often the police who set the partnership agenda. In American cities like Aurora and Chicago, the urgency of gang-related violence was such that the harmfulness of gang membership was largely taken for granted. As a result, the focus was not, as it is in France, on differentiating collective juvenile offending motivated by gang allegiance from differently motivated variants; where gang-related violence is rampant, the focus of American police is primarily on differentiating between those who can be rescued from involvement with gangs and those whose gang offenses can only be abated through enforcement action by the police. It is a triage, in many cases, between individuals, not between different forms of collective offending or different forms of gang activity. And where the focus is on gang-related violence, as it often is in the US, it is the police who take the lead in deciding when to resort to arrest and prosecution over preventive strategies aimed at peripheral members.

Yet despite these differences, we have identified the same five intelligence regimes and thus the same distinctive array of approaches to problems of collective juvenile offending in both the United States and France. Because they transcend national boundaries, we contend, these ideal types make it possible to identify commensurate units of comparison across very different policing systems. The notion of an intelligence regime in fact makes it possible to link cross-national with subnational comparisons of policing approaches and thus to identify affinities between the public safety approach of Chicago and Marseille and the features that bring these cities' approaches to problems of retaliatory youth violence closer to each other than they are to the rival approaches of other cities in their own countries.

This claim about ideal-typical similarities between French and American knowledge communities makes us splitters at the subnational level and lumpers across national borders. A single site in either country will display all five distinct intelligence regimes and different cities within the same country will vary enormously in their approach to any given problem, depending on which intelligence regime is tasked with taking the lead in addressing it. At the same time, comparisons across commensurate intelligence regimes (such as the partnership intelligence regime in Aurora and Nantes) help bring out what features the partnership intelligence regime has in common across national borders. In both France and the United States, addressing juvenile crime involves efforts to disentangle different strands of collective juvenile offending and assigning each to the most suitable regime; and it also involves the selection of one or more dominant regimes; efforts to coordinate the selected regime(s) with the others; and efforts to do so in ways that create synergies rather than conflicts, as discussed later.

5 The Five Intelligence Regimes

Table 1 provides an ideal-typical overview of the five intelligence regimes in French and American law enforcement agencies, as developed inductively from the authors' fieldwork in the United States and France.

5.1 Criminal Intelligence

5.1.1 Regime Categories

Aims: Investigators seek to identify offenders, build cases, and search for admissible evidence. The relevant unit is the case.

Main Actors/Network Participants/Ecology of Actors: The primary actors who use criminal intelligence and evaluate the means by which it is collected are criminal investigators (detectives in the US, judicial police in France) along with crime analysts, prosecutors, and judges (including investigative judges, in France). The wider audience also includes trial judges, defense attorneys, and crime victims, as well as jurors (including lay and professional judges sitting together in the French court of assizes).

Time Horizon: This intelligence regime is backward-looking to offenses that have already been committed, planned, or attempted.

Professional Skills and Interpretive Lenses: Competent actors must have some knowledge of criminal law and criminal procedure, be trained investigators, and be able to assess what makes information admissible evidence in the criminal process.

Criteria of Relevance: Information is relevant if it is material to guilt or innocence or establishes incriminating links between distinct offenses and offenders.

Criteria of Validity: Information has validity if it has probative value as evidence or leads to the discovery of information that counts as evidence. In France, this means it belongs in the case file; in the U.S., this means it will be admissible at trial.

Criteria of Importance: Information in this regime is important if it concerns a serious offense or links multiple offenses into a series.

Information, Knowledge, and Understanding Being Sought: Intelligence must fit into the categories of criminal law and procedure and must be or lead to admissible evidence.

Table 1 French and American intelligence regimes summarized

	Public Safety Intelligence PS1	Partnership Intelligence PI	Criminal Intelligence CI	Order Maintenance OM	Managerial Intelligence MI
1 – Aims	– Policing public protest – Avoiding violence, disruptions in public realm – Anticipating size of police presence that will be necessary – Identifying & monitoring threats to public safety	– Deliberating about problems of shared concern – Agreeing on a plan of action, dividing up & coordinating tasks – Expanding repertoire of approaches/ solutions	– Identifying offenders – Gathering admissible evidence (building cases) – Criminal prosecution	– Addressing petty crime, quality of life issues, neighborhood conflicts, hot spots, open-air drug markets – Responding to situations that call for immediate action (calls for service)	– Setting enforcement priorities, defining long-term objectives, and matching problems with intelligence regime(s) best capable of handling them – Optimizing & shifting resources to their best use
2 – Main Actors/Network Participants (Ecology of Actors)	– Political authorities – Intelligence units/ analysts – Rapid intervention teams – Criminologists – Developers of predictive algorithms	– Participants in local security partnerships; Community policing officers – Those who can marshal specialized expertise may prevail over those with more institutional power – Police decentered – Housing, education, transport and municipal officials	– Detective units/police judiciaire – Prosecutors – Probation officers and French equivalents	– Patrol units - – Community policing officers – First responders, mediators	– Political leadership – Command hierarchy – General staff and their analysts – Consultants, outside experts, e.g. in ILP

Table 1 (cont.)

	Public Safety Intelligence PS1	Partnership Intelligence PI	Criminal Intelligence CI	Order Maintenance OM	Managerial Intelligence MI
3 – Types of Information, Knowledge, Understanding That Is Being Sought	– Social, historical & economic context of a movement, group, or organization; membership change over time – Predictive Insights, e.g. through erstwhile Bui Trong algorithm in France, SSI algorithm in Chicago	– Co-produced multidisciplinary – Reduced to a common denominator – Determined by interests & concerns of the partners	– Must fit into categories of criminal law & criminal procedure – Must be or lead to evidence – Focus on past or recent past (e.g. flagrant offenses)	– Situation: sense of street-level actors – Subjective – Tacit knowledge, difficult to transmit – Focus on immediate problems, the present	– Search for evidence-based approaches to maximizing efficient use of police resources in relation to public safety problems – Guidance from criminology & organizational theory – How well different units perform
4 – Time Horizon	Future	Variable–depends on partners' concerns	Backward-looking	Present	Variable: focus on change over time
5 – Criteria of Relevance of Information	– Predictive utility – Confidentiality/ secrecy/publicity can be managed – Whether information is checkable	– Information reflects the views of influential partners – Whether partners can agree on its usefulness for addressing a problem – Information is within the purview of at least one partner's responsibilities	– Legal categories govern – Information is admissible evidence or leads to it or – Bears on guilt or innocence of a suspect, or helps link offenses or offenders	– The information attracts attention of ground-level actors as requiring immediate action	– A theoretical framework treats the information as relevant to police performance; it is countable & can be aggregated with other, similar data

Table 1 (cont.)

	Public Safety Intelligence PSI	Partnership Intelligence PI	Criminal Intelligence CI	Order Maintenance OM	Managerial Intelligence MI
6 – Criteria of Validity of Information	– The information has a reliable, credible source; has been corroborated; – The information facilitates deployment of rapid intervention teams or other preventive action to abate risk	– Consensus among partners that the information is valid – The criteria of validity are negotiated	– It is corroborated by admissible evidence – It counts as reliable under rules of evidence and criminal procedure	– It is treated as reliable by ground-level actors, often without opportunity to check it out; reliance on rules of thumb and prior professional experience	– Methodological rigor (according to external theoretical framework) of the way the information was gathered and analyzed, coherence with theoretical Framework.
7 – Criteria of Importance of Information	Gravity & urgency of the threat, the degree to which it calls into question the governing capacity of the political leaders and command hierarchy	– It has been debated & evaluated collectively – Agreement that it matters	– It links multiple offenses into a series – It concerns a serious offense – It belongs in the case file, has probative value – It is important to obtaining a conviction	– The ground-level actors who gather the information consider it important – It is transmitted to higher officers in the chain of command or requested by them	– Information is not important on its own; it is simply data to be aggregated; only the trends & patterns that emerge from statistical analysis are treated as significant

Table 1 (cont.)

	Public Safety Intelligence PS1	Partnership Intelligence PI	Criminal Intelligence CI	Order Maintenance OM	Managerial Intelligence MI
8 – What Professional Skills Are Useful to Analysts	– Social science training – Writing ability – Training in using predictive software – Strength in building one-on-one relationships with sources	– Expertise in situational crime prevention & in subject areas of common interest to partners, – Expertise in statistical methods, survey research – Skill in setting agenda, keeping minutes, and following up with partners	– Knowledge of criminal law & procedure – Investigative skills; Turning information into evidence; – Connecting related crimes & offenders recruiting informants – The case method remains dominant	– Situation sense, ability to assess risks & dangerousness of individual situations – De-escalating conflicts, mediation; – Rapport with residents, skill at connecting with people from all walks of life	– Knowledge of organization's record-keeping apparatus, skill in aggregating such data & mapping trends over time
9 – Action Repertoire Which Intelligence is Supposed to Support	– Deploying order maintenance units – Negotiation – Disruption – Orienting the search for further intelligence – Mediating between protest groups and authorities	– Partner's own repertoire of interventions – Coordinated with institutional partners – Collective action & partnership governance – Social support, job training, mentorship through nonpolice actors – Opinion surveys	– Trial – Criminal investigation – Coercive measures	– Reassurance of public – Public presence – Responding to calls for service – Addressing local quality of life concerns – Stopping crimes in progress & making arrests	– Strategic planning – Selecting regimes to take lead in addressing a problem – Coordinating regimes – Managing the flow of demands on police resources – Allocating resources – Evaluating performance

The professionalization of criminal intelligence analysis has only brought the French and American variants of the criminal intelligence regime closer to each other. So-called "link analysis" reveals connections between seemingly disparate offenses and offenders by linking people, things, locations, money flows, and crimes. This is a tactic first developed in the English language literature[42] and then applied in the United States, the UK and, more recently, in France, where the Rennes Gendarmerie, for example, used link analysis to trace international capital flows to organized shoplifting, which investigators thereby elevated to the manifestations of organized crime.[43]

An analyst from the Rennes Gendarmerie who uses link analysis to put together complex investigations of organized crime reported that "I always point out the weak parts in the case file, verbally, when I put my report in the case file ... I write white papers that suggest leads to follow, and which leads should be given priority," which phones are the most promising ones to monitor, and how to dismantle a network most effectively when the time comes to make an arrest. "We had a transporter who worked for two separate [drug] distribution rings, and the investigators had to choose which of them to arrest, and I wrote a white paper advising them on which was the most promising one," based on the evidence that had been obtained so far. "The analyst can set the limit for how many people to arrest ... based [on the analyst's assessment] of the importance of the target and the strength of the evidence."[44]

In Aurora, Illinois, a shared database of 600 to 800 active gang members allowed investigators to discern patterns and links which in turn determined which subset of targets were best investigated for murder; which should be pursued for racketeering; and which could be investigated primarily for drug sales. Seeing the connection between offenses and offenders also made it possible for the chief and the federal task force to select the most promising targets and to decide which offenses to focus on and how to describe the racketeering enterprise that held the individual offenses together, making it possible to join all the defendants as part of a pattern of racketeering activity for which the gang members could be held responsible collectively.[45]

---

[42] R. V. Hauck, H. Atabakhsh, P. Ongvasith, H. Gupta, & H. Chen (2002), COPLINK Concept Space: An Application for Criminal Intelligence Analysis, *IEEE Computer Digital Government* 35(3):30–37; M. K. Sparro (1991), The Application of Network Analysis to Criminal Intelligence: An Assessment of the Prospects, *Social Networks* 13(3):251–274; www.fmsasg.com/linkanalysis/LawEnforcement/GangActivity.asp.

[43] Interview with analyst for the National Gendarmerie's "section de recherche," Rennes, Winter 2014.

[44] *Ibid.*

[45] Interviews with Aurora PD delegate to ATF gang task force for Aurora, Aurora PD chief, Aurora PD analysts, and lieutenants, Summer 2008 and Summer 2009.

Action Repertoire: Criminal intelligence culminates in searches, seizures, and arrests, paving the way for the collection of more evidence to build a criminal case. Techniques like link analysis help prosecutors to tie cases together for indictment and trial. This technique also helps investigators to pinpoint the locations they should search first, or which persons they should arrest simultaneously, to maximize the evidentiary yield and to identify key figures in criminal networks and gangs.

5.1.2 Criminal Intelligence and Collective Juvenile Offending: Comparing the United States and France

In the United States, where the criminal intelligence regime has long been a dominant approach to the problem of gang violence, a significant strand of legal and policing scholarship addresses the pros and cons of prosecuting street gangs as racketeering enterprises.[46] Saul Bernstein, for example, sees criminal prosecutions as the most promising way of countering the social pathologies associated with gang violence. Bernstein suggests that the police "break up larger and more destructive gangs" by incarcerating their leaders, because this encourages gang members "to adopt quieter and less visible ways of expressing their impulses."[47] Bernstein claims that prosecutions aimed at the destruction of the most powerful and violent gangs feeds a trend toward "smaller and less formal groups," which, he assumes, would reduce the overall level of violence. His approach resonates with state and federal task forces which have used the RICO statute to go after the leadership of street gangs.

Cities like Aurora, Illinois, followed a well-trodden path when they doubled down on RICO prosecutions of warring gangs. In Aurora, in the early 2000s, the concern with collective juvenile delinquency was essentially a concern with gang violence, which was itself fueled by competition over turf in the sale of drugs. In an effort to dismantle Aurora's most lethal street gangs by removing their leadership, the Aurora Police Department, under Chief Greg Thomas,[48] worked closely with the Bureau of Alcohol, Tobacco and Firearms (BATF), the Drug Enforcement Administration (DEA), and the Federal Bureau of Investigation (FBI) to build racketeering cases against the Latin Kings and the Insane Deuces,

---

[46] L. S. Bonney (1993), The Prosecution of Sophisticated Urban Street Gangs: A Proper Application of RICO, *Catholic University Law Review* 42:579–613; J. Wheatley (2008), The Flexibility of RICO and its Use on Street Gangs Engaging in Organized Crime in the United States, *Policing: A Journal of Policy and Practice* 2(1):82–91; J. B. Woods (2002), Systemic Racial Bias and RICO's Application to Criminal Street Gangs and Prison Gangs, *Michigan Journal of Race and Law* 17(2):303–357.

[47] S. Bernstein (1964), *Youth on the Streets: Work with Alienated Youth Groups*, New York: Association Press.

[48] Greg Thomas was chief from 2008–15.

targeting them as criminal organizations.[49] During its own racketeering prosecutions of powerful street gangs, in the 1990s, the Chicago Police Department had laid the groundwork for such prosecutions by assembling a specialized database just for local gangs, using field contact reports from police stops of gang members to record which gang members were seen with which associates, when, where, and in which cars, to posit connections between offenses.[50] The premise of such databases, like the premise of Aurora's racketeering prosecutions, was that gangs were by their very nature criminal organizations.

By contrast, French sociologists like Marwan Mohammed and Laurent Mucchielli differentiate between spontaneous assaults or thefts committed by individual gang members and those attributable to street gang collectively.[51] Gangs, these authors contend, often take the place of families and serve as a locus of solidarity and friendship, not just crime. Mohammed and Mucchielli refer to these gangs as "bandes de jeunes," or youth gangs, to distinguish them from "bandes de crime organisé," or criminal organizations, as the term "bandes" can create confusion as applied to what the authors view as very different types of entities. A number of French judicial officers who specialize in the investigation of organized crime likewise insisted on the need to distinguish between gangs and local drug organizations that employ young people who happen to be gang members.[52] These investigators were far more willing to deploy the criminal intelligence regime against local drug organizations than against street gangs. In France, which has no equivalent to RICO and no tradition of prosecuting gangs as forms of organized crime, sharp distinctions between gangs and criminal businesses makes it possible to treat collectives of young drug dealers as members of criminal organizations, according to the norms and expectations of the criminal intelligence regime, without treating youth gangs themselves as criminal organizations, even if their memberships overlap.

In the north of Paris and Marseille, chiefs of intelligence units who monitor local gangs reported (in 2017) that outbursts of violence between rival gangs in their respective cities are rarely planned and rarely concern disputed drug locations, while many drug traffickers who do kill each other during turf battles belong to criminal organizations that are more like businesses than street gangs.[53] "We don't have Chicago-style gangs," a supervisor of a criminal

---

[49] Interviews with Aurora PD delegate to ATF gang task force for Aurora, Aurora PD chief, Aurora PD analysts, and lieutenants, Summer 2008 and Summer 2009.

[50] Interview with gang prosecutions investigator in the CPD, Fall 2009.

[51] M. Mohammed & L. Mucchielli, eds. (2007), *Les bandes de jeunes: Des blousons noirs à nos jours*, Paris: La Découverte.

[52] Interviews with French organized crime investigators of the DIPJ, Marseille and Versailles, Fall 2017.

[53] Interviews with judicial police analysts and supervisors, Versailles and Marseille, Fall 2017.

intelligence unit in Marseille reported. "A network is a business, hiring employees, [and] there's no hierarchy. There are no gang colors, and there's no neighborhood loyalty." The bosses who run the business hire young people from outside the neighborhood, the supervisor reported.[54] Retailers are "recruited to sell for a day and only know the person who recruited them. The organization might keep him for fifteen or thirty days; but he's only paid by the day."[55] Instead of gangs, intelligence supervisors asserted, the bosses of Marseille's syndicates are heads of competing crime families. Marseille's criminal organizations are anchored by family ties, intelligence supervisors report, not by gang affiliation.

One organized crime expert within the National Police questions whether local street gangs and drug dealing organizations can be so neatly distinguished. "The political authorities don't want to stigmatize gangs by labeling them organized crime, particularly since no-one really knows to what extent they are involved in criminal activity on an organized basis and to what extent drug networks coincide with gangs."[56] In his view, however, treating the phenomena as distinct allows the judicial police (who investigate serious crime) to concentrate on the overseas links of organized crime, while leaving local gang crime to the Public Safety Police.

There are some indications, however, that the French legal system has begun to encourage the police to investigate gangs as criminal collectives, and as manifestations of organized crime, while proscribing other, lesser form of collective offending. Legal reforms have introduced new offenses such as "participating in a group for the purpose of preparing acts of violence and the destruction of property."[57] The law of March 2, 2010 also expanded the criminal association offense to include a variant that can be committed by juvenile street gang; and the Penal Code imposes penalties of up to five years' imprisonment for armed groups who wear masks to hide their identity or who instigate armed gatherings.[58] Alongside the new criminal prohibitions, the June 16, 2021 government plan "to prevent violence by gangs and informal groups"[59] called

---

[54] Interview with supervisor of DIPJ, Marseille, Fall 2017.   [55] *Ibid.*
[56] Interview with organized crime analyst for National Police, Fall 2017.
[57] Penal Code article 222–14–2 introduced by loi n. 2010–201 of March 2, 2010, "reinforcing the fight against group violence," provides for up to one year's imprisonment and a 15,000 Euro fine for participating in a group preparing for physical violence and the destruction of property.
[58] Penal Code article 431–4 al. 2, 3, 5, 6.
[59] The inter-ministerial plan to prevent violent crime by gangs and informal groups, issued on June 16, 2021 calls for prosecutors to apply older laws to violent collectives. The relevant offenses include offenses committed by an "organized gang," as defined in article 132–71 of the French Penal Code, and criminal association, defined by article 450–1 of the Penal Code, as well as violations of article 24 1° loi du 29 juillet 1881, which proscribes the instigation of criminal conduct.

for prosecutors to apply existing criminal laws to violent groups, whether these were deemed street or organized crime.[60] Ambushing the police and other public authorities now carries lengthy prison terms.[61] In 2011, a legal reform established new correctional tribunals for minors over the age of 16 who qualify as recidivists; the new courts are designed to be more punitive than the more lenient youth courts established in 1945 with a mandate to educate and reform juvenile offenders.[62]

Noting the political appeal of crime-fighting solutions, Teillet[63] documents legal changes that have turned criminal prosecution into a more powerful tool for incapacitating particularly violent or prolific members of juvenile collectives, whether they commit crimes in temporary groupings or in more established gangs. For Sauvadet,[64] the enactment of these laws marks the criminalization of juvenile rites of passage that were once tolerated as ephemeral excesses. Jacques de Maillard, however, views some of these reforms as largely symbolic and sees little application of the new laws to juvenile offenders.[65] A number of commentators have documented abusive police practices and conflictual interactions between police and juveniles on the ground, against members of formal or informal gangs.[66]

In Marseille, which has experienced a growth in retaliatory violence between competing drug trafficking organizations, the Prefect of Police has been encouraged by the new penalties to create a task force of public safety and judiciary police, to overcome the rift between those who investigate street gangs and those who investigate organized crime. According to a supervisor in the Direction Interregional de Police Judiciaire in Marseille, his unit worked with

---

[60] Article 24 1° loi du 29 juillet 1881 carries up to five years' imprisonment for gang members who call for violence; see also including article 222–11 of the Penal Code, which calls for enhanced punishment of violent crimes linked to gangs. Article 222–11 of the Penal Code, modified by Ordonnance n°2000–916 du 19 Septembre 2000 – article 3 (V) JORF 22 Septembre 2000 en vigueur le 1er Janvier 2002.

[61] Article 222–14–1 du Code Pénal Version en vigueur depuis le 27 mai 2021; modified by loi n°2021–646 du 25 mai 2021 – article 51.

[62] Loi du 10 aout 2011.

[63] G. Teillet (2015), Cinq Années de Guerre Contre les Bandes: Processus de Renforcement d'un Arsenal Répressif Ciblé, *AGORA débats/jeunesses* 70:79–94.

[64] T. Sauvadet (2006), *Le Capital Guerrier, Concurrence et Solidarité entre Jeunes de Cité*, Paris: Armand Colin.

[65] J. de Maillard (2010), Les Politiques de Sécurité, in O. Borraz & V. Guiraudon, eds., *Politiques Publiques 2: Changer la Société*, Paris: Presses de Sciences Po, 57–77.

[66] M. Boucher, M. Belqasmi, & E. Marlière (2013), *Casquettes Contre Képis: Enquête sur la Police de Rue et l'Usage de la Force dans les Quartiers Populaires*, Paris: L'Harmattan, 448; E. Marlière (2007), Les "Jeunes de Cité" et la police: de la Tension à l'Emeute, *Empan* 67:26–29, https://doi.org/10.3917/ethn.084.0711; F. Ocqueteau (2008), Violences en Actes dans les Rapports entre Mineurs et Policiers: Sortir d'une Impasse Théorique et Pratique, *Archives de Politique Criminelle* 30:149–162; F. Jobard (2021), Policing the Banlieues, in J. de Maillard & W. G. Skogan, eds., *Policing in France*, New York: Routledge, 187–201.

criminal investigators who "go to buy drugs abroad, and then [we investigate] the chain of distribution."[67] At the same time, information from street-level units "helps us see what families are emerging as dominant, who's in charge of the organization."[68]

The professionalization of criminal intelligence analysis has thus brought the French and American variants of the criminal intelligence regime closer to each other. Nonetheless, the US is more apt than France to treat street gangs as organized crime and thus to deploy link analysis and its analogues to both and to characterize both as "racketeering enterprises."[69]

5.2 Public Safety Intelligence

5.2.1 Regime Categories

Aims: Unlike criminal intelligence, public safety intelligence is about predicting future events, abating threats, managing risks, and disrupting plots against the state or challenges to the state's authority. This paradigm has traditionally been used to forestall violent protests or riots, to disrupt terror plots, or to track the evolution of social movements that challenge state control over public spaces. It has often been used for domestic intelligence operations, which Samuel Rascoff describes as proactive efforts to "make sense of information about a hazard before the underlying risk materializes."[70] Applying this paradigm to gang-related violence is relatively new in both the US and France, where such approaches have been tried in Chicago and Marseille, respectively.

The Main Actors and Network Participants (the Ecology of Actors): Prime actors include intelligence analysts who identify and evaluate threats and members of the general staff (and their political bosses) who identify politically salient threats to public safety as priorities.

Time Horizon: The focus of this predictive regime is the future, as intelligence is used to select an abatement strategy and to allocate resources accordingly.

Professional Skills and Interpretive Lenses: Analysts who study the composition and evolution of protest movements, religious and political organizations, gangs, and criminal organizations often have a social science background and a working knowledge of statistics, and sometimes a training in predictive algorithms. These analysts are judged by their ability to aggregate and analyze bulk data, to identify trends, and to anticipate catastrophic incidents before they

---

[67] Interview with DIPJ supervisor (for organized crime), Marseille, Fall 2017.   [68] *Ibid.*

[69] Interview with supervisor of an Illinois fusion center, Fall 2015.

[70] S. J. Rascoff (2010), Domesticating Intelligence, *Southern California Law Review* 83:575–648, 585.

occur, not by their skill in bringing offenders to justice or building criminal cases. Analyses delve into the social, political, ideological, and economic contexts in which events such as protests, gang conflicts and terrorist attacks must be situated for better understanding and for the design of an effective response. Like domestic intelligence operations, the information collected about public safety threats is aggregative and "places a premium on the rigous analysis of data."[71]

Like criminal investigators, analysts must have some skill in recruiting informants and in knitting together a network of confidential sources inside or close to the monitored protest movements, gangs, terrorist organizations, or sports fan organizations. For this reason, the Chicago intelligence unit hired analysts whom a supervisor described as "seasoned police officers who [had] worked as patrolmen [and] have a strong connection to the areas they worked in."[72] In France, analysts must also be able to maintain ongoing relationships with institutional partners in religious organizations, sports stadiums, unions and schools, to monitor the evolution of the relevant organizations.[73]

Criteria of Relevance of Information: To be selected as relevant, information must either make it possible to predict or to monitor threats to public safety. Information is useful to public safety actors if it is checkable and if it can be kept confidential (or if the manner in which it is publicized or characterized can be managed).

Criteria of Validity of Information: To be considered valid intelligence rather than raw data, public safety information must be corroborated, usually by cross-checking tips against other information and by verifying the reliability of the source.

Predictive analysis is successful even when prevention fails. In discussing the predictive algorithm on which the intelligence unit relies in assessing gang members' risks of becoming a party to violence, in the fall of 2015, an intelligence unit supervisor from Chicago reported that "We include the score in the victim profile" [if the subject is later shot], and the supervisor of a fusion center that has access to these predictive scores recalled that officers routinely checked the "heat score" of anyone who was killed, and tended to view the fact that he had a high number as proof that the algorithm "worked," even though the preventive intervention it was meant to trigger did not[74] (see more below on Chicago's predictive algorithms).

---

[71] *Ibid.*　　[72] Interview with supervisor of Chicago PD intelligence unit, Fall 2009.

[73] Interviews with analysts of Renseignements Territoriaux in Bordeaux, Nantes, and St. Etienne, 2014 through 2017.

[74] Interview with supervisor of Chicago intelligence unit, Fall 2015.

Criteria of Importance of Information: Analysts judge the importance of intelligence by the gravity and imminence of the threat. The seriousness of the threat may be measured by the degree to which it calls into question the competence of political leaders and the command hierarchy. Marseille and Chicago developed public safety approaches to gang violence largely because of the political salience of gang violence, as reflected by media coverage. But threats to public may sometimes be symbolic (like the ransacking of the Tomb of the Unknown soldier during the yellow vest riots in Paris).

Types of Information, Knowledge, or Understanding Being Sought

The aim of this intelligence regime is to place current development in a broader social, historical, and economic context, so as to predict their future evolution. Analysts rely on information about various types of groups, including their dynamics and intentions, beliefs, and proclivities for violence; these can be terror groups, political movements, gangs, sports clubs, religious groups, or criminal organizations, if they pose potential challenges to political authorities or risk of a significant impact on the public realm.

Because the Chicago Police Department's intelligence unit is primarily interested in abating future gang violence, not in gathering evidence to prove past offenses, it uses a predictive algorithm that is meant to identify those most at risk of becoming victims or perpetrators. Working closely with criminologists from the University of Illinois at Chicago, the intelligence unit has compiled a Strategic Subject List (SSL) that assigns an SSL score to each person identified as a "strategic subject." A supervisor explained that the list assigns a score to each gang member to capture his likelihood of becoming a "party" to violence in the next six months.[75] The subjects' SSL score is updated daily, to take account of an incoming stream of intelligence that is considered valuable primarily because it can easily be standardized and amalgamated with other data in order to generate insights about shifting patterns of violence and the associated predictions of where and when gang-related violence will surge next.

In Paris, the Renseignements Territoriaux (who serve as the intelligence branch of the Public Security Police) likewise monitor the increasingly violent conflicts between rival street gangs in the north of the city to identify flashpoints and triggers for violence.[76] A gang analyst from St. Etienne reported that he sought to understand how the membership and demographics of a gang change

---

[75] *Ibid.*

[76] Interview with supervisor of what was then the Renseignements Generaux intelligence agency, Fall 2007.

over time, to predict what it will grow into, and, in particular, whether it is expected to radicalize politically or to veer into profit-driven criminal activity.[77]

Action Repertoire Which Intelligence Is Supposed to Support: Public safety intelligence often culminates in saturation policing through rapid intervention units, though it can also include efforts to disrupt violent networks, to negotiate with key figures, and to alert other units to the need for new sorts of information to watch out for.

In Chicago, for example, intelligence analysts helped supervisors to direct mobile saturations teams to the sites at which the next retaliatory shooting could be expected; for this purpose, the intelligence unit needed to understand the background behind each gang-related shooting.[78]

But in Chicago, predictive algorithms also fed into a complex carrot and stick approach to abating threats by gang members most at risk of killing or being killed. Prosecutors requested denial of bail when someone with a high "heat score" was arrested for an otherwise bailable offense. An intelligence unit supervisor reported that "if the person [who has a high heat score] is under arrest . . . the score can be introduced for enhanced charging and prosecution."[79]

The score is also used to try to shock those most at risk into changing their ways. The intelligence unit supervisor described a variety of efforts to use the scores to change behavior. "District management takes twenty [high-risk people on the list] and notifies them that they're gonna end up in jail or dead." The police accompany these warnings with an offer to "help you with housing, G.E. D. [a high school equivalency certificate], charities for clothing." But the carrot comes with a stick. "If you refuse [help], we'll come down on you hard. Any little thing you can be charged with, you will be charged with," and the police will seek enhanced parole conditions to maximize supervision. "We'll sit them down with parents and grandparents" to reinforce the message: "Stay off that corner, don't talk to any gang members."[80]

In France, too, analysts saw stark differences between the types of action that flow from public safety intelligence and those which are fed by criminal intelligence. Explaining the difference between intelligence work and criminal investigation, an intelligence analyst in St. Etienne reported, "the criminal investigators rely mostly on arrests, interrogation, searches, and wiretaps," which yield evidence for immediate use in a criminal prosecution.[81] By contrast, French intelligence units have limited investigative means at their disposal

---

[77] Interview with analyst of Sousdirection de l'Information Generale (a successor of the intelligence agency formerly known as the Renseignements Generaux).
[78] Interview with supervisor of Chicago intelligence unit, Fall 2009.
[79] Interview with supervisor of Chicago intelligence unit, Fall 2015.   [80] *Ibid.*
[81] Interview with intelligence SDIG analyst, Spring 2014.

because they have no coercive powers that would allow them to arrest or interrogate gang members in order to recruit them as informants, nor do they have significant sums at their disposal for remunerating informants with money instead of leniency. Their aim is not to "flip" gang members on their confederates or to gather evidence for criminal cases but to continually adjust their threat assessments in light of the patterns they observe in gang behavior. According to the St. Etienne analyst, "we can take a step back and take a longer-term perspective, do analyses of how the groupings we're interested in are changing over time."[82] Without the same coercive means at their disposal, intelligence agents are not expected to use arrests to alleviate the problems of a neighborhood. Instead, their task is to follow trends from a distance and alert the political authorities – including the director of public security police and the prefect – in order to facilitate strategic planning at the top of the command hierarchy. And when collective violence does lead to arrests[83] for undermining the security of the state, rioters may be charged with insurrection rather than gang violence, to reflect the public safety concerns of the authorities, as the French prohibition of insurrection applies even to "informal groups" that lack the permanence and structure of criminal organizations.[84]

Likewise, French intelligence analysts who seek to forestall violent conflicts between politically inflected soccer fan clubs in St. Etienne and Bordeaux reported that, while prosecutors were more than willing to sentence violent soccer hooligans to significant prison terms, building criminal cases was not what the analysts were trying to accomplish; their aim, instead, was to channel the enthusiasms of fan clubs into nonthreatening forms of expression, while sidelining only individual catalysts of group violence through stadium bans or criminal prosecution.[85]

5.2.2 Public Safety Intelligence and Collective Juvenile Offending: The US and France Compared

In the United States, where collective youth violence often involves confrontations between rival gangs, criminologists have documented and to some extended spurred the rise of a public safety paradigm for thinking about gangs. In consonance with the public safety regime's emphasis on prediction

---

[82] *Ibid.*

[83] These arrests would be made by other units cooperating with public safety analysts.

[84] Loi n. 2015–912 du 24 juillet 2015-article 2 (insurrection against state institutions); article 212–1 of the Penal Code, prohibiting "collective violence that violates the public peace"; loi 2 mars 2010, which proscribes intimidation by informal groups that take over common areas of public housing to control access by residents.

[85] Interviews with intelligence analysts for SDIG in St. Etienne and Renseignements Territoriaux in Bordeaux, 2014–15.

of future violence based on trendlines,[86] analysts who work within this paradigm sometimes use network analysis and mathematical models "to assess an individual's or group's probability of behaving in a certain way or becoming victimized by certain behavior." Algorithms for predicting retaliatory gang violence became a central preoccupation of police and criminologists alike, though commentators have criticized key assumptions behind this paradigm, along with the way in which it has been implemented.[87]

In Chicago and Marseille, analysts concerned with public safety have focused primarily on analyzing retaliatory violence between young people running competing open-air drug markets, to assess possible links to gang activity and to disrupt a cycle of escalating violence that has called into question the state's ability to govern, to control "its territory" – as suggested by public discussion of whether there are no-go zones in both cities – and the state's ability to enforce its authority in public spaces.

In Chicago, where gang conflict challenges successive mayors' ability to govern, Chicago reliance on federal racketeering prosecutions in the 1990s – then the city's dominant approach to gang violence[88] – gave way to efforts to anticipate gang-related violence and to disrupt the cycle of retaliatory shootings. Since 2001, therefore, the Chicago Police Department's intelligence unit treats the problem of gang violence not simply as a crime problem but as a public safety threat, like the riots for which French intelligence analysts developed their own predictive algorithm known as the "Echelle Bui Trong."

According to an analyst in the CPD's intelligence unit, predictions about imminent violent acts are based on "arrest records, crime records, calls for service." Gang-related shootings are broken down by district, so trends can be identified spatially through statistical analysis. Analysts combine the data with geographical information and map it out visually, to reveal, for example, "two gang locations and a conflict area in the middle, which overlaps with a spike" in the violence. "We use [the] intel to predict where the [next] crime I going to

---

[86] W. Sanders & S. Lankenau (2006), Public Health Model for Studying Youth Gangs Emphasizes "Examining a Youth Gang as Social Network," in J. F. Short, Jr. & L. A. Hughes, eds., *Studying Youth Gangs*, Lanham, MD: Alta Mira Press, 117-128, 126.

[87] M. M. Feeley & J. Simon (1992), The New Penology: Notes on the Emerging Strategy of Corrections and its Implications, *Criminology* 30(4):449–474; M. M. Feeley & J. Simon (1994), Actuarial Justice: The Emerging New Criminal Law, in D. Nelkin, ed., *The Future of Criminology*, Thousand Oaks, CA: Sage, 172–201; B. Harcourt (2007), *Against Prediction: Profiling, Policing and Punishing in an Actuarial Age*, Chicago, IL: University of Chicago Press.

[88] J. McCormack (1999), Winning a Gang War, *Newsweek*, October 31, reporting that "federal prosecutors had put away 80 of the gang nation's top operatives ... By early November, the Justice Department is expected to indict a new crop of about 20 GD's, and prosecutors promise still more indictments."

happen . . . .We use 911 calls about gang activity, about shots fired . . . we vet calls for what we want [i.e. information about shootings or gang members]."[89]

Due to concern with the limitations of predictive algorithms, supervisors ask analysts to supplement statistical data with "HUMINT" [human intelligence] to explain individual conflicts that sparked violence.[90] When there is a shooting "we try to get a subject profile on the victim; we have automated that..[We get] the victim history, criminal history, contact information from contact cards, his predictive score, and his gang affiliation."[91] Combining information about statistical trends and individual cases, the analyst reported, "we brief the command on each offender, victim, and [heat] score . . . three times a day," conducting both "a statistical analysis of the whole and a factual analysis of each case," in order to detect and explain patterns in what can be dozens of shootings in a single weekend.[92]

Starting in 2012, Marseille, too, mobilized its public safety regime to "take back control of the streets" from local drug trafficking organizations after an increase in retaliatory violence by drug trafficking organizations feuding over turf. A period of intensive surveillance of open-air drug markets was followed by targeted sweeps of basements and other common areas where guns and drugs were stashed.[93] Afterward, the CRS – France's anti-riot police – remained in the neighborhoods long enough to disrupt the operations of the city's main drug trafficking operations and to allow neighborhood organizations to reopen public spaces for family events and improvements to the infrastructure, alternating their interventions between neighborhoods of rival drug organizations to avoid having any one organization derive a benefit from the setbacks of its competitors. The sweeps did not result in significant criminal sanctions, but the subsequent occupation of the former open-air drug markets by riot police effectively disrupted the business of the leading organizations, cost then money, and forced them to operate more discreetly.[94] But while Chicago tried the public safety approach after the perceived failure of the criminal intelligence model, which did not decrease gang-related violence despite the mass incarceration of gang members, Marseille's subsequent efforts to step up the collection of criminal intelligence to build cases against the city's top drug dealers are, at least in part, a response to the mixed record of the city's earlier efforts to implement a public

---

[89] Interview with CPD intelligence analyst, Fall 2015.   [90] *Ibid.*   [91] *Ibid.*   [92] *Ibid.*

[93] Interviews with Marseille general staff, Renseignements Territoriaux, partnership liaisons, commanders who coordinated with CRS (anti-riot police used to conduct sweeps of neighborhoods with open-air drug markets), and commanders of other front-line units, Spring and Summer 2015.

[94] *Ibid.*

safety approach to the very visible presence of drug organizations in the public realm, and the associated violence.[95]

But the public safety regime also took special forms in Marseille, where the pélice mobilized a unit known as the Unité de Prévention Urbaine (UPU), or the urban prevention unit. This was a plainclothes unit whose members functioned as mediators and were fixtures on the streets of the most troubled Marseille neighborhoods. When there were incidents that threatened to give rise to riots – like an accident in which a police car accidentally ran over and killed a child – mediation officers described organizing a protest march on behalf of the victim's families, to stave off a more violent reaction by neighborhood residents. The mediation staffers organized the funeral and acted as liaisons between the police, the victim's family, and neighborhood residents, to reassure angry friends and family of the deceased that the incident would be thoroughly investigated.[96]

Though officially a mediation unit, the UPU doubles as an intelligence unit, reporting directly to the chief of the Public Security police in Marseille. According to a supervisor of the DIPJ (the regional Judiciary Police), "the UPU is very good on retaliatory shootings. It gives us information on neighborhood ambiance, but also names of people involved [in the shootings]. It predicts the outbreak of wars between drug organizations and it succeeds in calming things down. They know all the criminals since birth."[97]

The French public safety approach to juvenile offending, however, long predates concern with gangs or drug-trafficking organizations. French concerns about collective juvenile offending came to the forefront in 1995, with the outbreak of street riots by young people in the large cities of France. This spurred police efforts to classify urban disorders according to how directly they challenged the authority of the state.[98] In both Paris and Marseille, the Renseignements Territoriaux investigate gangs not primarily as a criminal phenomenon in its own right but as a window onto other forms of collective youth action. Accordingly, rock throwing and vandalism were of interest primarily as weak signals of impending riots. That a particular outbreak of violence was sparked by a chance encounter between rival gangs is often registered as an indication that the police are *not* witnessing the outbreak of a riot aimed at the state.

---

[95] Interviews with judicial police supervisors, Spring 2015 and Fall 2017.

[96] Interviews with commander and members of UPU, Spring 2015.

[97] Interview with commander of DIPJ, Fall 2017.

[98] The algorithm used for this was called the "Bui Trong scale," after the police commissioner who invented this early predictive algorithm for the French intelligence services, in 1991. L. Bui Trong (2000), *Violences Urbaines: Des Verites Qui Derangent*, Paris: Bayard.

According to Mohammed and Mucchielli,[99] however, it was the nationwide street riots of fall 2005 that first made the interdiction of urban street gangs an urgent public safety concern, even though the role that street gangs played in the relatively spontaneous eruption of violence remains highly disputed. The Prefecture of Police established a permanent working group to monitor gangs and gang-related violence in the greater Paris area, which gathers intelligence about gang hierarchies and leadership and monitors gang activity in real time through specialized maps and surveillance teams.[100]

In France, public safety intelligence thus targets many potentially explosive forms of collective action by juveniles in settings other than street gangs. In Paris and St. Etienne, public safety concerns involving young people coalesce around riots, student protests (which frequently draw students from lycées, or high schools), and violent clashes between soccer fans, while intelligence analysts follow simmering gang conflicts at some remove to ascertain how gang membership and gang activities change over time.[101]

Nonetheless, French intelligence agencies in the northern districts and suburbs of Paris also follow the gradual emergence of youth gangs that derive their group identity from the housing developments in which they live. An intelligence supervisor who followed public disturbances and their ties to street gangs in the north of Paris reported that gangs regularly do battle with rivals from neighboring housing development. "They'll meet in a shopping center, parking lot, or major avenues near McDonald's, and there will be a fight, in which they attack each other with iron bars, knives, and baseball bats, maybe a hundred people at a time."[102]

To disrupt escalating cycles of violence between gangs, intelligence officers of the Renseignements Territoriaux seek to identify the causes, the triggers, and the dynamics that lead to escalation. "The same middle schools and lycées enroll students from lots of different housing developments," the same intelligence supervisor explained,

> "and we have fights that break out between gangs from rival towers. In one recent school fight we had three students injured. We used to think the gangs cohered around the schools they attended, but students now identify much more with the developments in which they live, and now they throw bottles of acid on each other in the hallways, and flammable liquids, sometimes even in the middle of class. We don't really know what's driving it, it seems to be

[99] Mohammed & Mucchielli, *Les bandes de jeunes*, 13.
[100] www.lagazettedescommunes.com/813934/a-paris-une-cellule-bande-pour-lutter-contre-les-rixes/.
[101] Interview with supervisor of what was then the Renseignements Generaux Seine St. Denis, Fall 2007; interview with analysts for the SDIG, Spring 2013.
[102] Interview with supervisor of the Renseignements Generaux, Fall 2007.

a rejection of the whole system, and sometimes it's gang members who come in from the outside, who don't go to school there."[103]

In contrast with the algorithmic approaches increasingly favored by the American police, French analysts' work on gangs and local drug trafficking networks is folded into the larger task of monitoring "the life of a neighborhood ... the atmosphere, how people feel about their neighborhood, the opening of new businesses, what young people are up to more generally, any worrying increase in the number of car burnings, fights between groups of young people, but also conflicts between rival businesses, hang-outs and hot-spots, and any increase in religious sectarianism."[104]

What Chicago's approach to gangs shares with the French approaches described above is a commitment to the public safety paradigm. One indication that Chicago's new approach to gangs should be situated in the register of public safety intelligence is the extent to which the Chicago intelligence unit redeploys many of the technologies it developed for the surveillance of protest movements and uses them, with the same public safety orientation, to identify links between gang members who are known to be involved in violence, to assist in predicting and suppressing future outbreaks. For example, analytic software that was acquired to monitor networks of regular protesters is being redeployed to monitor gang members instead. A supervisor in the Chicago intelligence unit reported that "we have a small group of officers monitoring labor protests but [that is] not a big problem here. We use [the program] more for gang violence than for protests, except the NATO summit," for which the analysts used it as well.[105]

Reliance on so-called targeted response units also echoes peacekeeping tactics. A supervisor described the rapid intervention units as "a supplemental force for large scale events, such as election night ... to deal with large crowds," and as "trained in civil unrest tactics and procedures." These units were used to support a "terrain-centered" strategy designed to saturate neighborhoods where retaliatory shootings were expected, in order to "make it hard for individuals to move around, especially in their cars, which have guns in them ... Suppressing movement in cars [means gang members] can use guns less. We go after gangs [when we] suppress their business and their enforcement tool ... tamping down on retaliatory shootings."[106] This approach supplemented the use of "heat scores" to identify gang members most at risk of killing or being killed, and to intervene through a mix of offers of help and threats of incarceration. That this was an effort to head off spiraling violence can be gleaned from the focus on

---

[103] *Ibid.*   [104] Interview with supervisor of SDIG of St. Etienne, Spring 2013.
[105] Interview with analyst of CPD intelligence unit, Spring 2015.   [106] *Ibid.*

those gang members who were deemed most at risk, rather than those with lower "heat scores" who were most likely to accept an offer of help and most likely to change their ways.

What unites public safety intelligence in both countries is a focus on predicting future trajectories of ongoing conflicts; containing escalation; and on saturation tactics designed to reassert police authority over public space in ways previously reserved for public protests and riots.

5.3 Order Maintenance Intelligence

5.3.1 Regime Categories

Aims: Order maintenance intelligence is what frontline officers employ to triage and assess situations that call for some immediate decision about whether and how to respond. When officers address some form of collective action by juveniles, the focus is not only on crime but on quality of life issues and nuisances that generate complaints from residents about overt signs of neighborhood dysfunction, including open-air drug markets, fights, the takeover of common areas by groups of juveniles who may not necessarily be members of a street gang, noise, graffiti, and vandalism. Order maintenance officers in France also responded to complaints about motorcycle racing ("rodeos"), while American officers responded to homeowners' fear of the degradation of their neighborhoods' housing stock and property values.

The Main Actors and Network Participants (the Ecology of Actors): Order maintenance intelligence is often generated by and for those who will need it in the field, as well as their direct supervisors. Supervisors provide first responders with guidance on what to look for, how to react, and what to pass along to the chain of command. A secondary aim is to secure the cooperation of outside actors who are also potentially a source of intelligence for the police.

Accordingly, order maintenance intelligence is not primarily the purview of intelligence units but of ground-level actors inside and outside the police. Within the police, these include patrol officers, surveillance teams known as anti-crime brigades in France, and emergency response units. In the US, community policing officers participate both in order maintenance and in partnership intelligence, frequently going back and forth between these twin roles. Outside of the police, the wider ecology of actors includes community residents, and school, transport, and housing officials, along with mediators, social workers, and the members of the public who interact with first responders. These bilateral interactions with frontline officers take place outside the context of partnership deliberations and need not involve community policing officers or partnership liaisons.

In the United States, the relevant ecology of ground-level actors also includes private sector actors alongside police, municipal workers, and the like. The chief of a Midwestern fusion center reported that he regularly conducts what the chief described as "public safety outreach," advising a mall management company about how to distinguish ordinary fights from those motivated by gang membership. Gang fights were more likely to escalate and more difficult to defuse, he explained, potentially requiring earlier requests for police assistance than the ordinary scuffles which mall security officers are trained to disrupt.[107]

Within higher police echelons, the ecology of actors who evaluate the information received from first responders and residents, as relayed by ground-level actors, includes sergeants and lieutenants – middle management personnel – who must discern trends and patterns in local occurrences and must decide how to interpret them, what to do about them, and what resources, if any, to mobilize in response.

Time Horizons: If criminal intelligence pursues evidence of past crimes and public safety looks to future hazards, the order maintenance regime focuses primarily on frontline actors' decisions about how to respond to situations requiring some immediate decision on their part about whether and how to react in the present, in light of supervisory guidance on how to handle certain situations and what information to be on the lookout for. The relevant unit of analysis is the situation, not the criminal case or the threat.

Professional Skills and Interpretive Lenses: Ground-level actors must determine how to classify a problem and benefit from knowing their neighborhood and the people who live there. They must grasp the problems of foremost concern to residents, be familiar with local trouble spots, and be able to spot telltale indicators that something is wrong or that someone needs their intervention. Supervisors, in turn, must be able to provide intelligence to frontline personnel about whom and what to look out for while ensuring that matters of interest are transmitted back from the front lines to middle management.

In Aurora, Illinois, police on the streets had to be able to recognize and to teach others how to recognize the signs of gang activity.[108] And the midwestern intelligence chief who counseled mall security on how to recognize signs of gang conflict sought to give those on the scene the tools to displace a conflict, to safeguard the physical space, to protect shoppers, and to decide when to involve the police.[109] In the suburb of Cenon, near Bordeaux, first responders had to ascertain whether the motivations behind a harassment campaign against local

---

[107] Interview with supervisor of a Midwestern fusion center, Fall 2015.
[108] Interviews with community-oriented policing officers, Summer 2008 and Summer 2009.
[109] Interview with supervisor of a Midwestern fusion center, Fall 2015.

merchants was gang-related. This required a close relationship with local merchants and immediate follow up on incidents to differentiate among the motivations among overlapping groups of juveniles.[110]

Criteria of Relevance of Information: The order maintenance regime rests on the situation sense and accumulated experience developed by ground-level actors and must respond to calls for service and assess problem situations in the immediate present, based on limited information that may be augmented by electronic notifications to hold someone for questioning. Information is relevant to the extent is assists them in performing this initial work of classification and triage.

The police captain in Cenon who used his patrols to investigate harassment of local merchants gave out his cellphone number of local merchants, treating the information they gave him as relevant if it could be used to provide the merchants with some respite from harassment, by furnishing a lead that could be acted on immediately, or by facilitating a seizure of contraband or arrest in the immediate aftermath of a crime.[111] In contrast to traditional intelligence units, the captain rarely had time to search for corroborating intelligence before taking action to reassure the victims. But the stops and identity checks of suspects right after an incident provided the captain with an opportunity to update his knowledge of which juveniles were involved in which types of illegal activities and with whom.[112]

In Aurora, first responders also needed to assess calls about gang- and drug-related locations so they would know how to react in real time, often by being told whether the location was known for similar complaints, or whether violent incidents at that location was likely to be gang-related. Information about calls for service at houses known for gang or drug activity was considered relevant if it could be aggregated, quantified, and linked to related incident reports, because patterns of gang-related violence at any given location could generate expulsions of gang members or legal action against landlords.[113]

Criteria of Validity of Information: Information counts as reliable if it is treated as such by ground-level actors, even if they often lack the opportunity to check it out. The information that ground-level actors share is often anecdotal and decontextualized. In Chicago and Aurora, however, ground-level actors are also asked to prepare field contact reports that standardize and summarize their

---

[110] Interview with commander of front-line units, Cenon, Winter 2015.
[111] Interviews with Cenon captain and the commander of front-line units, Cenon, Winter 2015.
[112] *Ibid.*
[113] Interviews with Aurora's community oriented policing officers, Summer 2008; ride-along and interview with an Aurora community oriented policing officer, Fall 2009; interviews with Aurora lieutenants and Aurora police chief, Summer 2008.

contacts with persons of interest who are often signaled to them in bulletins asking them to keep an eye out for particular people or phenomena.[114] Ground-level actors often perform identity checks and stop-and-frisks because these generate the kind of information about the encounter with suspected gang members that can be fed into keyword searchable gang databases, in the case of Chicago, or into activity reports perused by Aurora's lieutenants when they search for patterns in the reported criminal activity in their area. Identity checks perform a similar intelligence role in France, where first responders generated incident reports called *mains courantes*.

In Cenon, the validity of information was assessed according to the captain's rapport with the victims. Background information was judged useful if it revealed a possible motivation for the incident and reliable if it came from victims who had previously reported similar incidents that had been corrobor-ated by a follow-up investigation.[115]

Criteria of Importance of Information: The Cenon captain viewed youth harassment of local merchants as a serious problem because it created a climate of fear among merchants and residents and because the closure of the businesses would have signaled a further disintegration of the neighborhood's social and economic infrastructure. In Aurora, calls for service from homes associated with gang activity were treated as important if they signaled the occurrence of shootings, generated frequent complaints from neighbors, or were discussed by residents at beat meetings.[116]

In particular, information counts as important if it requires the person who collects it to take immediate action, and if a ground-level actor or supervisor considers it essential to making a decision about how to classify a problem and how to address it in the immediate present. Information is also considered important if it appears to be the kind of information that supervisors have asked ground-level actors to look for (through bulletins and briefings) or that will be fed into databases and aggregated.

Types of Information/Knowledge/Understanding Being Sought: In Aurora, the patrol division geared its ground-level operations to gathering intelligence about what the gangs were doing and where they were doing it.[117] Patrol units were directed to park their cars at suspected drug locations whenever they drafted police reports inside their vehicles. The chief equipped patrol officers with digital cameras, so they could send images of graffiti to the lieutenant, who

---

[114] Interview with gang prosecutions specialist for CPD, Fall 2009; interviews with Aurora police chief and Aurora lieutenants, Summer 2008.

[115] Interview with Cenon captain, Winter 2015.   [116] *Ibid.*

[117] Interviews with Aurora police chief, lieutenants, and crime analyst, Summer 2008.

used the graffiti to collect intelligence on the evolution of the gangs. Patrol officers were instructed to view their interactions with residents as opportunities to learn more about ongoing gang activity and to pass these insights along to commanders. Aurora's community oriented policing officers, too, were responsible for keeping track of their neighborhood's problem locations, for example, by responding to calls for service whenever the call came from one of the places they were already monitoring, so that they could query possible links to evolving gang conflicts or known gang members in their district.[118]

In Cenon, the captain directed rapid intervention units to respond immediately to reports of harassment, so they could identify the juveniles involved and learn more about the background of the incidents.[119] His aim was to differentiate, in real time, between the intimidation of merchants who did not want to assist drug dealers in laundering drug proceeds; threats meant to drive out nonhallal businesses; and harassment designed to extort money from merchants or to protect (or shift) a drug dealer's retail operations, by driving out non-cooperative businesses and replacing them with fast-food operations that could serve as hangouts and lookout spots for drug dealers. Part of what he sought to determine was whether the juveniles' gang affiliation was a factor.[120]

Action Repertoire: In both countries, directed patrols of identified "hot spots" are a favored tactic against open-air drug markets. In Aurora, police also monitored the locations were known gang members lived, to generate information that could be used to enforce housing ordinances against landlords who rented to gang members. In one such case, a lieutenant reported, "we learned that no background check had been done [on the residents] and we had the city send the landlord a nuisance abatement notice, [warning him] that [official] action could be taken because he had not done a proper background check" on his tenants, whose gang-related activities repeatedly generated calls for service at their apartment.[121] The French police lack this legal avenue against private landlords, and expulsion from public housing remains an exceptional remedy.

In Cenon, the shifting motivations behind the attacks were useful in selecting between a range of possible interventions. Every morning, the captain spoke to his neighborhood sources in order to find out where incidents were clustering and in order to identify key players, so the police could determine whether to search for offenders, protect a particular location, or shut down a particular open-air drug-dealing hot spot.[122]

---

[118] *Ibid.*

[119] Interviews with Cenon captain and commander of street-level units, Winter 2015.

[120] *Ibid.*   [121] Interview with Aurora police lieutenant, Fall 2009.

[122] Interview with Cenon captain, Winter 2015.

5.3.2 Order Maintenance: French and American Approaches Compared

A significant strand of U.S. and French scholarship about gangs aligns with the order maintenance regime by identifying those internal gang dynamics that have the most negative impact on neighborhood life, fanning fears and complaints that lead to calls for service to the police. Marwan Mohammed[123] identifies the dynamics by which the pursuit of in-group cohesion leads to conflicts with outsiders. Spergel and Curry[124] (1990) viewed crackdowns by order maintenance officers as unavoidable for members of "racket"-oriented gangs that are "integrated into the criminal life of a neighborhood" and members of "theft"-oriented gangs that have a predatory relationship with local inhabitants, but he viewed less confrontational police tactics as promising for "conflict-oriented" gangs that are disruptive to their communities but can benefit from legitimate outlets for their energies.

And in both countries, the conflictual relationship between police and juvenile groups – whether street gangs, rioters, or soccer fans – reinforce some of the order maintenance problems that patrol and rapid response teams are supposed to counter. Fassin,[125] Roché,[126] and Jobard[127] trace the increase in open conflict to the French government's abandonment of community policing in 2003, which, in Jobard's view, led regular battles with the police to become a primary motor by which young people situated themselves socially among their peers. For Juhem,[128] Mauger,[129] Poliak,[130] and Gaubert,[131] identity checks (which are akin to stop-and-frisk interactions in the US) fuel a siege mentality among young people who come to perceive the police as a rival gang contending for control over the same territory. A number

---

[123] M. Mohammed (2011), *La Formation des Bandes*, Paris: Presses Universitaires de France.

[124] I. Spergel & G. D. Curry (1990), Strategies and Perceived Agency Effectiveness in Dealing with the Youth Gang Problem, in C. R. Huff, ed., *Gangs in America*, Newbury Park, CA: Sage, 288–309.

[125] D. Fassin (2011), *La Force de l'Ordre: Une anthropologie de la police dans les quartiers*, Paris: Le Seuil.

[126] S. Roché (2006), *Le Frisson de l'Emeute: Violences urbaines et banlieues*, Paris: Le Seuil.

[127] F. Jobard (2006), Sociologie politique de la racaille, in H. Lagrange & M. Oberti, eds., *Emeutes Urbaines et Protestations, une Singularité Française*, Paris: Presses de Sciences Po, 58–80.

[128] P. Juhem (2000), "Civiliser" la banlieue: Logiques et conditions d'efficacité des dispositifs étatiques de régulation de la violence dans les quartiers populaires, *Revue Française de Science Politique* 50(1):53–72.

[129] G. Mauger (2006), *L'Emeute de Novembre 2005: Une révolte Protopolitique*, Bellecombe-en-Bauge, Paris: Éditions du Croquant.

[130] G. Mauger & C. Fossé-Poliak, Les loubards, *Actes de la Recherche en Sciences Sociales* 50:49–67.

[131] C. Gaubert (1995), Badauds, manifestants, casseurs: Formes de sociabilité, éthos de virilité et usages des manifestations, *Sociétés Contemporaines* 21:103–118.

of American scholars (Meares, Tyler and Fagan,[132] as well as Tyler, Schulhofer and Huq[133]) echo these concerns about order maintenance tactics, noting that stop-and-frisk tactics undermine community trust in the police, without which police are unlikely to receive the cooperation they need from local communities in order to counter gang violence effectively.

In the US, order maintenance draws on community policing initiatives that France lacks. In Aurora, community policing helped to make order maintenance more proactive, as "community oriented police" served not only as liaisons to beat meetings but also as order maintenance personnel who could respond to calls for service and work closely with patrol officers and special operations units to address problems at particular locations, including drug-dealing and gang-related violence.[134] Working closely with middle management, they could develop proactive problem-solving approaches at the local level and call on the resources of criminal investigators to conduct surveillance, execute search warrants, and make undercover drug buys at problem locations. According to a supervisor, proactive investigations often begin when there is "a house where cars were coming and going all hours of the day and night. We suspected drugs and got information from different sources. We checked water billing, the tax assessor [to try to find out who lives there] and if we stop someone [coming from the house] we might try to work him for an undercover buy" [i.e. have him purchase drugs undercover from the house] or have an undercover agent from the special operations group make a drug buy from that location. The aim would be to build probable cause for a search warrant, so they could seize onsite drugs and expel tenants for gang and drug activity.[135]

The abolition of community policing in France in 2003, however, meant that French liaisons to security partnerships could not call on patrol or detective resources as their American counterparts did, because these liaisons did not straddle the partnership and order maintenance paradigms as their American counterparts did. As a result, French partnership liaisons could not themselves respond to calls for service nor call on criminal investigators to make arrest at open-air drug markets and other high-crime hot spots.

In Cenon, France, where the order maintenance regime encountered intimidation and extortion of local shopkeepers by juveniles, police questioned the

---

[132] J. Fagan, T. Tyler, & T. L. Meares (2016), Street Stops and Police Legitimacy in New York, in T. Delpeuch & J. Ross, eds., *Comparing the Democratic Governance of Police Intelligence*, Cheltenham: Edward Elgar, 203–231.

[133] T. Tyler, T. Schulhofer, & A. Z. Huq (2010), Legitimacy and Deterrence Effects in Counterterrorism Policing: A Study of Muslim Americans, *Law and Society Review* 44(2):365–401.

[134] Interviews with Aurora "community-oriented policing" (C.O.P.) officers, Summer 2008 and Summer 2009; interview with special operations lieutenant, Summer 2009; ride-along with Aurora C.O.P. officer, Fall 2009.

[135] Interview with Aurora lieutenant, Summer 2009.

contribution of gang affiliation to the problem, unlike police in Chicago and Aurora. The captain who oversaw the investigation of harassment incidents in Cenon concluded that these offenses were the work of overlapping groups of juveniles acting from diverse motives. Some wanted to drive out liquor stores or nonhallal butcher shops. Others extorted protection money. Yet others sought to take over a restaurant adjacent to an open-air drug market.[136]

In Aurora, triage performed by middle management focused on extracting peripheral members from gangs;[137] in Cenon, middle management sought to differentiate between multiple ongoing patterns of collective intimidation carried out by groups of young people. Among the motivations for the harassment campaigns, gang affiliation appeared to play a negligible explanatory role. But in both cities, the focus of the order maintenance regime included the full traditional range of ground-level interventions, such as the deployment of rapid response teams, stopping juveniles for identity checks, catching them red-handed in a drug sale, and making arrests.[138] In both Cenon and Aurora, surveillance of open-air drug markets was a favorite enforcement tool, though the Aurora police preferred undercover hand-to-hand drug buys to third party surveillance, which the Cenon police conducted from behind tress while camouflaged as shrubs.[139] Order maintenance intelligence was about responding to complaints from local residents about recurring situations that required some form of analysis and a patterned and immediate response.

5.4 Partnership Intelligence

5.4.1 Regime Categories

Aims: In both the United States and France, local security partnerships are heterogeneous intelligence regimes that deliberate about security problems of shared concern and that function as knowledge communities unto themselves. Deliberations are uniquely collective and multilateral. In ordinary interactions between police and their sources, it is the police who set the agenda, and sources will rarely know what others have told the police. In the partnership context, deliberations are open and each side will be privy to the contributions of the others and may challenge the analyses offered by police and other partners.

The objectives for which information is gathered are negotiated collectively and the police must sometimes yield sway to outsiders in defining matters of

---

[136] Interview with Cenon captain, Winter 2015.
[137] Interviews with Aurora C.O.P. officers, Summer 2008 and Summer 2009.
[138] Interviews with Cenon captain and Cenon commander of front-line units, Winter 2015; interviews with special operations lieutenant in Aurora and Aurora police chief, Summer 2009.
[139] *Ibid.*

concern to the partnership. Division of labor between partners can be useful to the police when others are willing to shoulder a burden that otherwise would fall exclusively on the police. On the other hand, such coordinated action plans will fail when there's a breakdown in trust. In Chicago, for example, the police partnered for a while with a group of "violence interrupters" known as Ceasefire. According to a police official who worked closely with them, members of Ceasefire used to attend intelligence briefings about where the unit would be sending its mobile strike force, so that Ceasefire could coordinate these interventions with their own outreach to victims' families. The district commander would also inform Ceasefire of "the five top bad guys in the area . . . Ceasefire would come and get documentation" so they could develop their own intervention strategies in the entourage of these targets. According to the analyst, however, CPD stopped meeting with Ceasefire and sharing sensitive intelligence because "some Ceasefire gang members were being arrested for gun activity. We're now negotiating which information we give [them]."[140]

Main Actors/Ecology of Actors: In both countries, partnership intelligence includes institutional participants such as municipal services, housing officials, public transport officials, and school officials. Local security partnerships often include social workers, and members of nonprofit organizations take part in discussions of a neighborhood's security needs.

In the United States, these partnerships tend to involve members of the public and community activists, while their French counterparts usually include only other institutional actors, filtering community sentiment through their lenses, or relaying primarily the concerns of other professionals who work with local residents.[141] However, French cities like Rennes and Nantes now invite representatives of tenants' associations to participate in such partnerships and have begun to try out focus groups of "trusted citizens" (often nominated by the police themselves).[142]

Time Horizons: The relevant time horizons are variable and negotiated. They may be the present, the past, or the future, as determined collectively by the participants, depending on the nature of their preoccupations. Identifying and arresting the persons responsible for a crime spree will involve a focus on past offenses. Abating recurrent noise complaints about a particular location may require increased responsiveness to complaints when they are called in, thereby situating the relevant time horizon in the *immediate present*, to deal with an

---

[140] Interview with CPD intelligence official, Fall 2009.
[141] T. Delpeuch & J. E. Ross (2017), The Co-production of Security in the United States and France, *American Journal of Criminal Law* 44(2):187–216.
[142] Interviews with Rennes and Nantes municipal security liaisons, Spring 2014.

ongoing nuisance. But troubling trends in teen behavior may also draw attention to what can be done to change behavior *going forward*, or to the need to prosecute local ringleaders for *past* offenses that have alarmed neighborhood residents.

Professional Skills of Participants: These are diverse, since participants have very different professional and educational backgrounds and invoke different forms of expertise. Partnership deliberations often call on agenda-setting skills by partnership coordinators within police or municipalities,[143] along with expertise in situational crime prevention, in the statistical analysis of crime data, in survey methodology, and in subject areas of common interest to the partners, such as psychiatry, education, and social work. Institutional players outside the police supply a range of expertise in urban design, survey methodology, social work, and conflict mediation, drawing on fields that are relatively unfamiliar to officers embedded other intelligence regimes.

Criteria of Relevance: It is ultimately up to the partners to decide whether to interpret and address particular disturbances – including petty offenses, drug use, and loitering by gang members – as crimes requiring police intervention; as public health concerns requiring medical intervention; or as social problems requiring conflict mediation. What information counts as relevant and credible is subject to negotiation, as are the criteria of success in addressing a problem. In Redon, where the Gendarmerie and mental health workers set up a plan to protect children from PTSD, Gendarmerie officers and health professionals exchanged information about children both as victims and as witnesses to violence. Information was relevant if it bore on the child's risk of reproducing traumas the child had witnessed, regardless of whether anyone was charged.[144]

In Aurora, too, the police role in partnerships was sometimes very different from that of criminal investigators who collect evidence for criminal prosecutions. Partnership liaisons gave a series of presentations about gangs to community groups and asked parents to contact them privately if their children were involved with gangs.[145] In contrast with criminal investigators, the partnership liaisons who follow up on reports about recently recruited gang members were mainly interested in loosening the gang's hold on peripheral members – not in turning the youngsters into informants. Detectives are ordinarily more interested in high-ranking gang members, who have access to more valuable

---

[143] In Grenoble, the same municipal security liaison attended separate partnership meetings of "security professionals" and "prevention professionals," to bridge the institutional divide between police and social workers, as the latter did not want to be seen to be communicating publicly with the police. Interview with Grenoble municipal security liaison, Spring 2008.

[144] Interview with Gendarmerie officer in charge of patrol, Redon, March 2015.

[145] Interview with Aurora C.O.P. officers, Summer 2008 and Summer 2009.

intelligence. But for partnership liaisons, information about gang member is of particular interest if their membership is recent enough to increase the chance of disentangling them from the gang.[146]

Criteria of Validity: Information is judged to be valid if the partners can agree on its validity. In Lyon, France, in fall 2007, during partnership deliberations about how to deal with young people loitering at the entrance to public housing, a housing official stated, to the nodding assent of the others at the round table, that whatever decision they all agreed on would be the right decision for the neighborhood "because if all of us agree to it, that's what makes it right." The emphasis is on procedural fairness as a source of legitimacy for agreed interventions.[147]

Criteria of Importance: These too are the negotiable; no partner monopolizes the definition of the subject matter for discussion. Topics can include all manner of security threats, large and small – from crime waves and vandalism to gang conflict and parking – but partnerships often focus on quality of life concerns, which may not figure prominently in crime statistics or in the performance indicators of the police, but which matter a great deal to local residents. Information is judged to be important if it has been debated and evaluated collectively; if the problem is of special concern to at least one of the partners; and if the partners agree that collective deliberation can improve the way in which the underlying problem is handled.

Types of Information: Analyses are co-produced, multidisciplinary and are usually influenced by the diverse interests and concerns of the partners. Partnerships sometimes sponsor new types of analyses produced by outside experts, such as nongovernmental organizations that conduct opinion surveys about ordinary people's satisfaction with the police (as in Grenoble, France).[148] Partnerships often supplement official crime statistics with local crime observatories' incident reports and statistical data derived from fire departments, hospitals, transport, and housing officials (as in Montpellier, France).[149] In the US, outside experts sometimes include volunteer organizations run by crime-victims' families[150] and criminologists who use epidemiological approaches to advise police on how to abate violence among gangs (as in Boston[151] and Chicago[152]).

---

[146] *Ibid.*   [147] Statement made by housing official at partnership meeting in Lyon, Fall 2007.

[148] Interviews with municipal partnership liaisons for Grenoble, Spring 2008.

[149] Interview with director of Montpellier crime observatory, Spring 2008.

[150] Interview with Aurora Cares, Summer 2008; interviews with Aurora C.O.P. officers and Aurora police chief, Summer 2008 and Summer 2009.

[151] www.npr.org/2011/11/01/141803766/interrupting-violence-with-the-message-dont-shoot.

[152] Interviews with Chicago intelligence unit officers, Summer 2015.

In Aurora, community oriented policing officers sought information from community members about troubled buildings which attracted gang violence, cross-checking these locations against 911 records to determine which locations generated an unusual number of calls for service for crimes associated with gang and drug activity. The city then brought legal action to enforce housing ordinances against landlords who did not conduct proper background checks of their tenants and leased housing to known gang members.[153] Location-specific information was sometimes provided during partnership walk-alongs with the police.[154]

Local security partnerships in France occasionally inquire more deeply than the police into the background dynamics of activities that generate citizen complaints. In Nantes, for example, the mayor's office hired former intelligence agents from the National Police to address complaints about young people loitering in front of public housing. The intelligence agents, who had joined the municipality after the 2007 reform abolishing the Renseignements Généraux, undertook to analyze each such gathering spot in order to determine whether the young people involved were from the building or from elsewhere; whether they were truants or students who lack a venue for after-school activities; whether they were members of a gang; and, if so, whether they were mostly hanging out together near the place where they lived or using the location to sell drugs.[155] Municipal authorities partnered with the National Police, and with recreational centers, social workers, and housing officials to analyze local youth gatherings and to tailor solutions to their diagnoses for each location.

Action Repertoire: The repertoire of problem-solving approaches draws on each partner's established routines but also expands to allow the partners to call on new forms of expertise supplied by outside actors, such as volunteer "violence interrup-tors" (like Ceasefire in Chicago)[156] or nonprofit urban design specialists who have studied the relative effectiveness of different types of violence interrupters, known as mediators, (in Grenoble).[157] In Aurora, partnership deliberations were at the

---

[153] Interviews with Aurora C. O.P. officers, Summer 2008; walk-along with Aurora beat meetings, Summer 2008; ride-along with Aurora C.O.P. officers, Summer 2008; interviews with Aurora lieutenants, Summer 2008 and Summers 2009; interviews with Aurora municipality's housing enforcement officials, Summer 2009.

[154] Beat meeting walk-along, Summer 2009.

[155] Interviews with multiple top-level municipal partnership officials, Nantes, Fall 2014; inter-views with intelligence officials of the Renseigenements Territoriaux, Nantes, Fall 2014.

[156] https://theconversation.com/faith-based-violence-interrupters-stop-gang-shootings-with-promise-of-redemption-for-at-risk-youth-not-threats-of-jail-142449#:~:text=Preventable %20violence&text=Founded%20in%201999%20with%20Illinois,otherwise%20end %20with%20fatal%20gunfire.

[157] Interviews with Grenoble municipal security officials, Spring 2008, describing urban design specialists' study (and ensuing partnership deliberations) about whether it is more effective to recruit mediators from the neighborhoods in which they are deployed (which gives them social capital) or from outside (to avoid inadvertently recruiting members of local street gangs who may pursue their own agenda).

origin of the campaign against graffiti, allowing police to highlight how useful they could be to the public as intermediaries who could mobilize a response from city services.[158] Rapid action against graffiti could be portrayed as a visible sign of the partnership's efforts to do something about gangs. Likewise, in St. Etienne, the police liaison to the local security partnership brought one of the country's first legal actions against juveniles for takeover of common areas, to show that he was doing something about residents' complaints.[159]

Partnership deliberation can decenter the role of the police in defining security concerns and in coming up with solutions. The Chicago School System, for example, partnered with a former gang member who had written a book on how he left the gangs, setting up presentations of his book at schools in neighborhoods with a significant gang presence.[160] And the Aurora Police Department's police chief and its gang and drug unit worked closely with public schools and with Aurora Cares, a not-for-profit organization headed by the mother of a child killed by warring gang members.[161] The city helped Aurora Cares to disseminate and publicize a documentary made by the organization, at the initiative of the bereaved mother. The film was a video depiction of the impact of gang killings on families in Aurora, and the police department handed out a city services handbook at screenings of the documentary and at meetings of Aurora Cares, advising parents on whom to contact if their children were in gangs.[162]

In Nantes, the range of solutions to complaints about juvenile loitering included help with internships or jobs for older members of the group, while providing after school assistance to students who had nowhere else to go, or tutoring and mentoring to students who were cutting school.[163] If it first established that a loitering spot was primarily a site for illegal activities – and that these are part of an illegal business, and not incidental to ordinary socializing among teenagers[164] – the city offered some of the juveniles who

---

[158] *Ibid.*

[159] Interviews with the police liaison to local security partnership, municipal security officials, the director of Public Security police and his second-in command, intelligence analysts for "urban violence" in the St. Etienne office of the Sousdirection de l'Information Generale, the successor to the Renseignements Generaux, subsequently renamed the Renseignements Territoriaux, and the chief of detectives (Surete) in St. Etienne.

[160] Interview in Summer 2009 with former gang-member Roberto Renteria, co-author with Corey Michael Blake of *From the Barrio to the Boardroom,* 2nd ed., 2013, Deerfield, IL: Writers of the Round Table Press. Renteria partnered with non-profit organization Aurora Cares and with the Chicago Public Schools to win students away from gangs; interview with pastor of Apostolic Church of God, Chicago, Fall 2009.

[161] Interviews with founder of Aurora Cares and chief of Aurora Police, Summer 2009.

[162] *Ibid.*

[163] Interviews with multiple top-level municipal partnership officials, Nantes, Fall 2014.

[164] *Ibid.*

participate in these gatherings an opportunity to or build a soccer field in an empty area nearby, or plan communal events to bring families back into shared spaces and to create social interactions among different age groups;[165] but if the underlying activity was mainly drug dealing, the city called for surveillance and searches of common areas taken over by young people.

5.4.2 Partnership intelligence and Collective Juvenile Offending: The US and France Compared

The French and American literature on local security partnerships focuses on their emergence as part of the successive reform movements that introduced community policing and problem-oriented policing to American cities,[166] and, eventually, to France.[167] In other work, we have argued for viewing these partnerships as sites for the construction of a new more open model for democratic participation in intelligence analysis.[168] The United States and France differ, however, in the role which the police tend to play in these partnerships, with French police in some French cities having had to cede a great deal more power to nonpolice actors in the definition of crime problems and the development of new approaches than have their American counterparts.[169]

In France, partnership efforts to reclaim public spaces from gangs led to a variety of efforts to experiment with new, nonpunitive strategies. In Montpellier, in 2008, members of the local security partnership reported having implemented a theater project that reclaimed litter-strewn housing courtyards for community productions.[170] In Bordeaux and Nantes, in 2015, partnerships responded to complaints about loitering youngsters by offering teenagers the

---

[165] Interviews with Nantes partnership officials who worked out and implemented these recreational offerings, Fall 2014.

[166] W. G. Skogan & S. M. Hartnett (1997), *Community Policing, Chicago Style*, New York: Oxford University Press; J. Fleming & J. Wood (2006), Introduction: New Ways of Doing Business: Networks of Policing and Security, in J. Fleming & J. Wood, eds., *Fighting Crime Together: The Challenges or Policing and Security Networks*, Sydney: University of New South Wales Press, 1–14; J. Fleming (2006), Working through Networks: The Challenge of Partnership Policing, in Fleming & Wood, *Fighting Crime Together*, 87–115; R. A. W. Rhodes (2006), The Sour Laws of Network Governance, in Fleming & Woods, *Fighting Crime Together*, 15–34.

[167] T. Le Goff (2008), *Les maires, nouveaux patrons de la sécurité?* Rennes: Presses Universitaires de Rennes; S. Roché (2002), *Tolérance zéro? Incivilité et insécurité*, Paris: Odile Jacob; L. Bonelli (2008), *La France a Peur*, Paris: La Découverte.

[168] Delpeuch & Ross, The Co-production of Security; T. Delpeuch, R. Epstein, & J. E. Ross (2016), The Joint Production of Intelligence in Local Security Partnerships: French Initiatives in Local Risk Management, in Delpeuch & Ross, *Comparing the Democratic Governance of Police Intelligence*, 43–85.

[169] Delpeuch & Ross, The Co-production of Security.

[170] Interview with head of Montpellier partnership initiative that sponsored the theater project, Spring 2008.

chance to design and plant community gardens near the troubled site.[171] In a number of French cities, partnerships organize recreational offerings tailored to the age groups most represented in community complaints about loitering, as identified by statistics compiled jointly by the city, the national police, and the municipal police.[172] And in Rennes, partnership officials organize community cafes in the public spaces outside public housing projects, to reclaim spaces for families in the temporary respite from drug-trafficking that follows security sweeps of common areas for hidden guns and drugs.[173]

In Redon, the Gendarmerie's attempt to address childhood trauma was premised on close partnership between the Gendarmerie, psychiatrists, and public health officials whose deliberations led them to conclude that the appeal gangs held for young people was rooted in post-traumatic stress from childhood exposure to violence.[174] To address this risk factor, the partnership put together a mobile team of child psychiatrists, therapists, nurses, social workers, youth counselors, and gendarmerie officers trained in forensic interviews of minors, who would visit the homes of "at risk" children and adolescents in the immediate aftermath of incidents in which children witnessed domestic violence. The team offered child victims or witnesses psychiatric evaluation and psychological counseling, along with referrals for academic support, tutoring services, and legal aid for victims. The team also offered short-term placement in crisis care facilities that could evaluate the family situation and provide parents with counseling and support, regardless of whether the children involved were removed from the home.[175]

But in Marseille, as in Chicago, the dominance of the public safety regime tended to marginalize the nonpolice actors who took part in local security partnerships, which had no active role in devising the overall security strategy. Although the overall plan had called for the city to partner with police and other social actors to revitalize the suburbs in the immediate aftermath of the security sweeps, the city instead chose to allocate national development funds to the modernization of the port and the construction of a large maritime museum to attract tourists. According to a supervisor in the Public Security Police who had been responsible for coordinating the sweeps,

> "the plan was for the [the security sweep] to disrupt the trafficking networks and calm things down for long enough to make repairs to public housing, to redesign public spaces, and to reclaim many areas for reactional activities that

---

[171] Interview with head of Nantes partnership initiative that sponsored the community gardens, Fall 2015.

[172] Interview with Nantes partnership officials, Fall 2015.

[173] Interview with head of Rennes partnership initiative that sponsored the community cafes, Fall 2014.

[174] Interview with Gendarmerie officer in charge of the partnership initiative, Redon, March 2015.

[175] *Ibid.*

were supposed to be sponsored by neighborhood associations. But once the [mobile riot police] left a neighborhood, the city, the housing authorities, and the associations didn't follow up."[176]

Without improvements to social services and physical plant, the police reported, drug traffickers were able to return, adapt to the schedule of sweeps, and reclaim the relatively unaltered public spaces from which the sweeps had temporarily forced them to retreat. This eventually led the police to turn back to the criminal intelligence regime as the primary tool against drug trafficking networks.

In Marseille, one reason for weakened police collaboration with local security partnerships crime prevention initiatives was the reduced role of the Unité de Prévention Urbaine (UPU). Until the early 2010s, a former chief of the unit reported, the UPU had been active in directing partnerships between the police, the city, and local NGO's that developed after-school programs for teenagers in the city's restive suburbs. For a long time, the chief of the unit advised the prefect on which youth outreach and afterschool activities to fund.[177] This in turn gave the chief of the unit tremendous influence with the city's social workers and youth outreach organizations as well as direct access to information from and about the associations whose financing he influenced. In this way, he claimed, he could channel funds away from organizations that had become fronts for drug dealers. Once the UPU lost this influence on the prefect's funding decisions, his influence on partnership initiatives waned.[178]

In Aurora, by contrast, partnership intelligence remained an important prong of the police anti-gang strategy. Community police coordinated partnership with order maintenance intelligence to win back peripheral gang members, by meeting with family members of newer recruits linked to gangs by graffiti and partnership deliberations.[179] In Chicago, where the public safety paradigm was dominant, anti-gang outreach targeted only the hardest cases. The use of algorithms was a police-driven, citywide approach – not a negotiated neighborhood initiative. Once the partnership regime took a back seat to the city's public safety strategy, beat meetings began to serve as a venue at which the police could publicize a city-wide approach they had developed independently, without debating new policing approaches with neighborhood residents.[180] According to a supervisor of the city's intelligence unit, the city's saturation strategy (which belongs quintessentially to the public safety

---

[176] Interview with member of general staff of the Public Security police, Marseille, Spring 2015.

[177] Interview with chief of UPU, Marseille, Summer 2015.   [178] *Ibid.*

[179] Interviews with chief of Aurora PD and Aurora C.O.P. officers, Summer 2008 and Summer 2009.

[180] Interview with CPD district commander, Fall 2009.

regime) had meant that "gang members disappear and [the] community sees that . . . . We had community meetings to explain the strategy" and its aim of dissuading gang members from moving around in cars, or at least from bringing their weapons when they do so.[181] Conversely, the police had little interest in collecting information about local problems. According to a CPD research and development specialist who observed what the police department did with the information generated at beat meetings, the information residents relayed to the police are "little individual pieces and not part of the big strategic planning. CAPS [beat meeting] information is not being aggregated."[182]

And when police felt they lost control of the agenda of partnership deliberations, they sometimes stopped sharing information with outsiders. In Aurora, a community leader recalled that a human relations committee was formed in the early 2000s "to create better working relations between blacks, Hispanics, and the police."[183] The human relations committee was to be formed with six representatives of the city and five members of the community, with the mayor exercising a power over the selection of the five community members, who were nominated by churches and civic organizations. From a concern with gangs, the focus shifted to racial profiling and police brutality. "The human relations committee was [supposed to deal with] complaints against cops that discriminated, and against the city when the city discriminated," according to a community leader who helped found the committee. The committee proposed meetings with the police and the creation of an oversight board to investigate complaints about particular officers. "But the police refused ... The police didn't want an oversight board with subpoena powers. We didn't really push for that but some of the mayor's people did, to make it fail."[184]

5.5 Managerial Intelligence

5.5.1 Regime Categories

Aims: Managerial intelligence, finally, is in play whenever policy makers and analysts try to decide how to handle a problem like gang violence more effectively or efficiently. This intelligence regime also helps the command hierarchy to evaluate the performance of police units and to improve the use of police resources. The subject matter of this intelligence regime is therefore not only external but internal: the police itself. This is the domain most influenced by intelligence-led

---

[181] Interview with CPD intelligence unit supervisor, Fall 2009.

[182] Interview with CPD research and development specialist, Fall 2009.

[183] Interview with member of Aurora Quad Cities Urban League, Fall 2009.   [184] *Ibid.*

policing, understood as an effort to subject police operations to evidence-based policy-making based on scientifically tested approaches to security governance.[185]

The aims for which intelligence is gathered are descriptive, predictive, and explanatory. Managers seek out information to help them set enforcement priorities and to define medium and long-term objectives. This regime frames the performance indicators by which the actors in these other regimes are judged and coordinates the activities and resources of the other four regimes, in order to improve their effectiveness and create synergies between them. Most importantly, the managerial intelligence regime guides decisions by police command about which of the other intelligence regimes should be asked to take the lead in addressing a given crime problem and about how the other regimes should lend their support.

If Chicago's police leadership sought to develop information about what was driving gang violence and why the criminal intelligence approach was not working, French cities like Vitry-le-Francois pursued information about whether a dramatic increase in assaults from 2008 to 2015 was attributable to gangs or to some other collective dynamic.[186] As in Chicago, Gendarmerie analysts' in-depth investigation of this troubling phenomenon sought to help the command hierarchy to develop an effective strategy to counter the trend.

Main Actors/Network Participants (Ecology of Actors): Managerial intelligence, like public safety intelligence, is often collected and analyzed by units that are explicitly called intelligence units, which may process public safety intelligence but may also supply the command hierarchy with the information it needs to develop enforcement priorities and strategy. Accordingly, the relevant ecology of actors consists of analysts and management. In France, Public Security Departments of the National Police, which have their own intelligence units (the Renseignements Territoriaux) also have additional intelligence units responsible mainly for compiling Compstat like statistical data about crime rates, clearance rates, and the performance of different units within the police. In France, these were usually known as ULIS (Unite de Liaison et de Synthese). Marseille also had the Unité de Prévention Urbaine (UPU), which is an intelligence unit (in the guise of a mediation unit) that reported directly to the chief of police. Chicago had a research and development unit that sponsored studies about whether the public safety approach reduced gang shootings (and then shelved the ambiguous findings without releasing them).[187] The primary audiences are the decision-makers and managers who control the allocation of resources and the

---

[185]   J. H. Ratcliffe (2008), *Intelligence-Led Policing*, Cullompton: Willan.

[186]   Interviews with commander of the Gendarmerie "groupement" of the Marne, the commander of the Vitry company, the brigade commander in Vitry, and the gendarme analyst responsible for compiling statistics on assaults in Vitry, Winter 2015.

[187]   Interview with CPD research and development officer, Fall 2009.

definition of enforcement priorities, within the city and within the police. The primary producers of this sort of intelligence are trained analysts, consultants, and outside experts (like the University of Illinois at Chicago criminologists who developed the predictive algorithm, in Chicago).[188] The Illinois Fusion center's analysts also seek to make sense of changing crime rates, and especially of gang-related shootings.[189]

Time Horizon: Coordinating the work of the other four regimes and aggregating data continuously, this regime had no preferred focus on any particular time horizon. Members of the managerial intelligence regime coordinated the other intelligence regimes, however, and in weekly meetings of the general staff, the work of these disparate regimes was typically discussed in order of importance to the chief, with the most important intelligence regimes first in the order of business. In Bordeaux, for example, a chief of the Renseignements Territoriaux implicitly recognized these temporal divisions between different segments of the police apparatus. Tasked with setting the agenda for weekly meetings of the general staff, he organized the agenda around "the future, the present, and the past,"[190] which allowed him to begin each meeting with the predictive intelligence work of his own unit, which was largely focused on public safety and notified the police leadership of upcoming events, including protests and possible riots, which would require the allocation of increased manpower on the ground. Order maintenance concerns were discussed next, with a focus on the demands the police were facing in the immediate present, while discussion of criminal cases was relegated to the end of the meeting, as they bore mainly on past events (most weekly police meetings in other French cities started with homicides and other serious crimes, moving from the past to upcoming protests and other public safety challenges).

What Professional Skills Are Useful to Analysts/Interpretive Frames: Analysts benefit from specialized training in statistics, criminology, situational crime prevention, and the social sciences, more generally. In France, statistical analyses were used to compare one month's performance measures for any given unit to that of any other in the same division and to the performance of any given unit during the same month in previous years. Analysts in both countries had to enable the general staff to assess the effectiveness of the intelligence regime that had been given the lead in handling any given problem and to compare it to results of earlier strategic choices about which intelligence regime to privilege as a vantage point on a problem such as collective juvenile

---

[188] Interview with CPD intelligence unit officer, Spring 2015.   [189] *Ibid.*
[190] Weekly general staff meeting with Bordeaux Public Security police, Bordeaux, Fall 2015.

offending. Crime maps displayed the deployments of police units in relation to crime clusters to display the impact of police tactics on clearance rates, crime rates, violence prevention, service to the public, and other quantifiable criteria of performance.

Criteria of Relevance of Information: Information is deemed relevant if it has the potential to influence strategic decisions about enforcement priorities and about how to distribute responsibilities between the four other intelligence regimes. To guide such decisions, managerial intelligence also relies on internal performance indicators for feedback on the effectiveness of enforcement strategies. Information is relevant if it can be counted by quantitative performance measures on which managers rely to identify "underperforming" units, or units with excess capacity that can be raided to improve the efficiency of understaffed units.

But some departments also rely on qualitative performance measures. In Aurora, for example, the chief considered what happened at local beat meetings to be relevant to assessing the success of his anti-gang strategy. The chief reported, "originally, meetings started because of violence. 'I can't walk out of my house'. Then violence went down. But they still meet. [But now it's to discuss] noise, parking, speeding problems. Quality of life issues."[191]

In Vitry-le-Francois, information about the background dynamics of long-term spike in assaults was held to be relevant to the extent it helped the Gendarmerie colonel assess the congruence between the underlying crime problems and the resources and tactics he was deploying to address them. Learning that the underlying problem was not, as he had supposed, an increase in animosity between local street gangs or a turf war between rival drug dealers but a clustering of downtown bar fights among an older clientele, the commander was able to reorganize the staffing of his patrols and the ways in which they were deployed.[192]

Criteria of Validity of Information: Validity is attributed to patterns and trends that emerge from aggregating multiple data points over time. Intelligence must allow management to assess competing explanatory theories about changes in police performance; the influence of factors like gang membership on crime rates; and the effectiveness of current strategies for addressing these problems.

Criteria of Importance of Information: No single bit of information is important on its own; raw information is simply data to be aggregated. Only the trends and patterns that emerge from statistical analysis and multivariable

---

[191] Interview with Aurora police chief, Fall 2009.
[192] Interview with general staff of Gendarmerie at Vitry-le-Francois, Winter 2016.

causal hypotheses are treated as significant. These in turn matter to the extent they can inform a decision about which intelligence regime should be asked to take the lead in addressing a particular crime problem. In Chicago, partnership information about housing that sheltered gang activity had some value for the managers who were in charge of strategy so long as expelling gang members from housing could lead to placing such properties into receivership and then selling them, as part of a process of neighborhood gentrification. Until the 2008 recession, Chicago's Troubled Housing Initiative worked closely with the Community Investment Corporation (CIC) and Neighborhood Housing Services to take action against landlords who rented buildings to gangs.[193] The city would follow up when residents complained about such locations at beat meetings, sending inspectors to diagnose code violations, in order to place pressures on landlords to expel gang members or to sell their properties. But when the troubled housing task force fell on hard times after the 2008 recession, it became harder to find buyers for property in receivership, according to a commissioner who ran the task force.[194] Once the process of selling and renovating troubled housing stalled, police reduced their collection of location-related intelligence at beat meetings.[195]

Perhaps, too, the shifting patterns and citywide geographic scope of gang violence made the CPD less willing or able to address other problems raised in partnership meetings, or to fine-tune their interventions to the concerns of individual districts and neighborhoods, given that the rapid intervention teams on which the saturation strategy depended tended to range so widely across the city. Whatever the reason, the city has, over many years now, cut its funding for the CAPS (community policing) program, which reached a high of $12.5 million dollars in 1999. By May 2011, CAPS funding had fallen to $4.7 million. In 2010, then mayor Daley reassigned 111 CAPS officers to address the rise in gang-related violence, and cuts to budget and staff resulted in a dramatic drop-off of partnership meetings and attendance at those that were held.[196] These long-term trends suggest that the city's managerial leadership of the troubled housing initiative, which had sought to figure out how to target the city's resources to the most troublesome hot spots of gang activity, was no longer as committed to incorporating local neighborhood concerns into the city's overall strategy against gangs, once a citywide public safety strategy

---

[193] Interview with commissioner in charge of the city of Chicago's Troubled Housing Initiative, Fall 2009.

[194] Interview with commissioner of Chicago's Troubled Housing Task Initiative, Fall 2009.

[195] *Ibid.*

[196] www.chicagoreader.com/chicago/caps-cpd-community-policing-analysis/Content?oid=23635982.

was in place.[197] The importance managers accord to information reflects the command hierarchy's decision to emphasize some intelligence regimes (such as public safety intelligence) over others (such as partnerships).

In Marseille, too, the primacy of the public safety approach spearheaded by the police themselves left the municipality relatively disengaged from the partnership regime.[198] The police ascribed this to the unwillingness of the city and of local housing officials to invest resources in revitalizing the suburbs following security sweeps by the police – and to a decision by the city to prioritize the use of national funds for the renovation of the harbor and for the construction of a new maritime museum to attract tourists.[199] Local security partnerships de-emphasized experimentation with crime prevention strategies, clamoring instead for the return of mobile units to sweep common areas for guns and drugs, as residents became increasingly concerned about drug traffickers' use of high-powered rifles to settle internecine power struggles. Police, in turn, did not treat partnership deliberations as valuable sources of intelligence about organized violent crime by young people, instead prioritizing information that the police generated internally, through informants, through the mediation unit, and through wiretaps.[200]

Types of Information, Knowledge, Understanding Being Sought: Analysts work with data about the law enforcement's internal workings (numbers of units deployed, hours, sites of deployment) and police impact on the security environment (in terms of visible presence, numbers of arrests, clearance rates, and the like). But analysts who belong to the managerial intelligence regime are also responsible for tracking changes over time in complex groups like gangs, protest organizations, and soccer fan groups, to enable decision-makers to formulate causal hypotheses about the factors driving increases in gang violence and in other collective juvenile offending. In Illinois, this meant analyzing the role criminal prosecutions had played in fragmenting Chicago's street-gangs,[201] heightening conflict between them. Analysts in the CPD and in Illinois fusion centers also assessed the promise of predictive algorithms for identifying gang members most at risk of killing or being killed. In France, and northern Paris in particular, the managerial intelligence regime investigated whether increases in concerted violence by young people were due to gang affiliation, violent conflict

---

[197] *Ibid.*

[198] Interviews with public safety police general staff, members of judicial police task force dealing with retaliatory shootings, and partnership liaisons, Marseille, Fall 2014.

[199] *Ibid.*   [200] Interviews with judicial police officers, Marseille, Fall 2017.

[201] Interviews with CPD intelligence unit analysts and supervisors, Fall 2009; interview with supervisor of Illinois fusion center, Summer 2015.

with the police, competition between retail drug operations, lack of recreational offerings, or ethnic conflict.[202]

And in Vitry-le-Francois, in France, where the Gendarmerie tried to determine how to staff day and night shifts in order to address an upsurge in assaults, the commander asked his analysts to classify all assaults according to whether they arose from domestic disputes, fights between young people from rival suburbs, gang rivalries, turf disputes among rival drug dealers, or conflict over common areas and public space. The commander also asked analysts to differentiate among threats or insults, on the one hand, and the use of deadly force, on the other.[203]

Action Repertoire Which Intelligence is Meant to Support: Managerial intelligence guides strategic decision-making by high-level actors, along with the allocation of resources. Starting in 2001, for example, Chicago's police leadership made a strategic decision to privilege the public safety regime as part of a new strategy that placed greater emphasis on predicting and preventing retaliatory shootings than on large-scale prosecutions of the sort that had made the criminal intelligence regime the dominant means of fighting gang violence throughout the 1990s, even though police and prosecutors continued to compile lists of "top twenty" targets and to prosecute violent gang members.[204] The public safety approach led police to emphasize predictive algorithms coupled with saturation policing of neighborhoods where retaliatory violence was expected.[205] And management made efforts to harness the other intelligence regimes to its new public safety approach and to its overarching aim of preventing future violence. Prosecutors were asked to pursue known gang members for weapons offenses, in order to disrupt cycles of retaliatory violence.[206] Police informed judges of offenders' algorithmic "heat score" at the time bail was set and again at the time of sentencing, so the offenders' dangerousness could factor into the decision to detain them without bail, to set a high bail, or to sentence them near the top of the range.[207]

The order maintenance regime, in turn, helped to develop intelligence about the changing affiliations and movements of gang members, as analysts used field contact information generated by officers on the street to update analytic snapshots of ongoing gang conflicts.[208] The police consulted this database

---

[202] Interviews with supervisors at central command of Renseignements Territoriaux, Paris, Spring 2015.

[203] Interview with commander and general staff of Gendarmerie, Vitry-le-Francois, Winter 2016.

[204] Interview with CPD intelligence unit supervisor, Fall 2009.

[205] Interview with CPD intelligence unit supervisor, Summer 2015.

[206] Interviews with CPD gang prosecutions officer and CPD intelligence unit supervisors, Fall 2009.

[207] Interviews with CPD intelligence unit supervisor, Fall 2015.

[208] Interview with CPD gang prosecutions officer, Fall 2009.

whenever they investigated the background of a gang-related shooting, in order to determine when, where, and from whom retaliatory violence could be expected.[209]

In Aurora, Illinois, the chief of police instead selected a three-pronged strategy that emphasized the pursuit of criminal intelligence aimed at the top of the gang hierarchy; order maintenance through a hot-spots approach to houses where gang members congregated (based in part on order maintenance intelligence); and partnership initiatives designed to disrupt recruitment of new gang members and to supply order maintenance officers with community input on troubled housing.[210] The public safety regime had much less of a role to play in the overall anti-gang strategy. Lieutenants were the lynchpin between the simultaneous federal criminal investigation of both of the city's main gangs, the order-maintenance strategies that was aimed at disrupting the gangs' retail drug business, and the community policing officers who attended beat meetings and alerted parents to the signs that their children might be involved with a gang.[211]

In Vitry-le-Francois, management's analysis of the steady increase in assaults from 2008 to 2015 also had a direct impact on police tactics. When it turned out that most of the increase was attributable to increased domestic violence and to downtown bar fights between older drunks, not between competing gangs, patrols were redirected from the suburbs to the city center, and a new detective division was created to take over the investigation of domestic violence incidents, to free up first responders from paperwork, and to conduct the necessary follow-up investigation that would ensure that such cases were prosecuted.[212]

5.5.2 Managerial Intelligence and Collective Juvenile Offending: The US and France Compared

Managerial intelligence is a form of meta-intelligence produced by analysts who assist commanders in monitoring police performance and crime trends, while devising strategy and allocating resources accordingly. The command hierarchy uses managerial intelligence to coordinate the other four regimes, sometimes choosing to entrust its dominant strategy to a given problem to one regime – like the public safety regime for gang crime in Chicago – while subordinating the work of other regimes to the logic of the dominant regime,

---

[209] *Ibid.*
[210] Interviews with Aurora C.O.P. officers, Aurora police chief, and Aurora municipal housing code enforcement officials, Fall 2009.
[211] Interview with Aurora police chief, Fall 2009.
[212] Interview with Gendarmerie general staff, Winter 2016.

much in the way Chicago used the threat of prosecution for gun-related crimes to incapacitate gang members singled out by predictive algorithms.

Some of the scholarly literature about gangs echoes the managerial regime in pursuing analyses that draw on different forms of expertise and feed into different intelligence regimes, depending on the underlying classification assigned to a gang. Richard A. Cloward's and Lloyd E. Ohlin's account[213] of "conflict-oriented gangs" suggests the promise of a public safety analysis, while their accounts of "criminal gangs" call for types of expertise we associate with the criminal intelligence; "retreatist gangs" in turn call for the outreach efforts of the partnership regime.

In both the U.S. and France, managerial intelligence is in play whenever the authorities attempt to determine whether their approach to a given problem is working, and, if it isn't, why not; the focus was on riots in France and on gangs in the US. In France, the police intelligence agency formerly known as the Renseignements Généraux, part of which has since been reborn as the Renseignements Territoriaux, has long been responsible for monitoring riots, protests, strikes, national security concerns, along with other forms of collective unrest that may be considered "threats" to public safety and the authority of the state. "Urban violence," gangs, and soccer hooliganism were more recent additions to their public safety mandate.

But when the 2005 riots broke out and riot control tactics didn't appear to improve matters, political authorities sought managerial intelligence from the Rensengienements Generaux in order to decide whether to think about the rioters as political activists with whom the government could negotiate or whether instead to view them through some other interpretive lens, an intelligence supervisor in what was then the Renseignements Généraux reported.[214] He claimed to have alerted the political authorities to his concern that traditional public safety approaches were only exacerbating conflict with the rioters; and he reportedly informed the prefect that these riots could not be managed through mediation or negotiation with key figures, because he did not believe that the violence was orchestrated or that any key figures were in charge. "In a movement like that [of the rioters], nobody controls anything, not even the leaders. It was like the social movements in the universities [in 1968]. Nobody was leading the troops. There's no leadership because there's no single movement, no political consciousness, no shared experience [among the rioters]."[215]

The supervisor doubted that any one organization – even "AC le feu," which put out a manifesto – could speak for what he did not view primarily a political

---

[213] R. A. Cloward & L. F. Ohlin (1960), *Delinquency and Opportunity*, Glencoe, IL: Free Press.

[214] Interview with supervisor in the Renseignements Généraux, North of Paris, Fall 2007.

[215] This interview was conducted in the Fall of 2007, before the Renseignements Généraux were split, renamed, and succeeded by the Renseignements Territoriaux.

movement, and he believed that the institutional interests of the spokespeople increasingly diverged from those they claimed to represent as their political activism gave them a television platform and a personal stake in promoting their view of the conflict.[216] His own opinion about the underlying forces behind the riots was that the rhetoric of the Minister of the Interior and police tactics themselves had enflamed the riots, and he reported that neighborhood organizations contacted him regularly to ask whether he could send a message to police leadership asking them to get frontline officers to take a less confrontational approach.

At a time when nothing seemed to be working to abate the violence, and no one could agree on what was driving the riots, the supervisor in effect functioned as a member of the managerial intelligence regime, openly questioning the appropriateness of existing public safety frameworks as interpretive lenses for making sense of the 2005 youth riots, along with the effectiveness of the state's saturation tactics. Tasked with preparing regular diagnostic snapshots of individual neighborhoods while monitoring the evolution of gangs, the supervisor stepped outside the public safety paradigm to question whether they were witnessing changes in collective action by juveniles that might counsel shifts in strategy, either in the direction of criminal enforcement or in the direction of new preventive initiatives designed to strengthen the "collective efficacy" of a neighborhood's legitimate institutions.

This conflict with the national political leadership of Nicolas Sarkozy (then the interior minister) proved a turning point in the state's approach to collective juvenile offending, to use the broadest possible term for the wide range of phenomena the state sought to manage. Not only were the Renseignements Généraux themselves spliced into two separate intelligence agencies (with their direct successor, the Renseignements Territoriaux, losing some independence from the law enforcement arm of the police);[217] police leadership used intelligence about the underlying phenomena involving young people to break these concerns down into components and to delegate different forms of collective juvenile offending to different intelligence regimes within the police. The Renseignements Territoriaux inherited urban riots and soccer hooliganism and were asked to monitor the evolution of street gangs, particularly in the north of Paris. But other intelligence regimes were activated to apply their own interpretive paradigms and to use their own analytical practices and their enforcement routines. The criminal intelligence regime became a tool against gangs and organized crime, as criminal investigators brought criminal cases against

---

[216] *Ibid.*

[217] L. Bonelli, Domestic Intelligence and Counterterrorism in France, in de Maillard & Skogan, *Policing in France*, 234–252.

rioters who attacked the police; sought new sentencing enhancements against gang members; and obtained increased powers to use sophisticated surveillance tactics against organized crime.[218]

In the north of Paris, the order maintenance regime inherited different forms of collective juvenile offending, as ground-level officers were tasked with investigating and shutting down open-air drug markets, through joint surveillance with intelligence agents. The so-called "plan stups" ["drug plan"] – later rolled out on a nationwide basis, with particular emphasis on Marseille – was a form of hot-spot policing that targeted the retail drug trade that was disrupting the quality of life in particular micro-territories. In the north of Paris, it featured a fairly unusual degree of cooperation between local police and the Paris prefecture's Renseignements Généraux, who put informants they had recruited against radical Islamists to work monitoring the local drug trade in their neighborhoods.[219] The coordination between police and intelligence agencies against the underground economy in northern Paris augured both an experiment with order maintenance policing and a new form of cooperation between intelligence agents and regular police units, by which the leaders of the Renseignements Généraux in the Prefecture of Paris could demonstrate their usefulness to other intelligence regimes at a time when the Paris intelligence unit alone had been spared the sweeping reforms the Renseignements Generaux had undergone elsewhere in France. In other parts of the country, such as Nantes, Bordeaux, and St. Etienne, partnership intelligence was used to experiment with new ways of diverting young people from gangs and drug-trafficking organizations. During presidencies of Francois Hollande and Emmanuel Macron, the Ministry of the Interior reintroduced a variant of community policing (renamed the Police de Sécurité Quotidienne in 2017) and sought to embed these new community policing initiatives within reinforced local security partnerships; but these pilot projects were implemented in only a small number of high-crime areas, and for relatively brief periods of time.[220]

But it was the police and political leadership, relying on their own managerial intelligence resources, that ultimately came to view collective unrest among young people as too multifaceted – too different in origin and expression – to be consigned solely to the "urban violence" section of the Renseignements Territoriaux or to fall within the exclusive jurisdiction any single intelligence regime. From city to city,

---

[218] This was the so-called Loi Perben II of 2004, loi du 9 mars 2004, portant adaptation de la justice aux évolutions de la criminalité.

[219] Interview with Renseignements Généraux supervisor at Préfecture de Police, Spring 2008.

[220] L. Figaro (2017), *Gérard Collomb s'attelle à l'élaboration de sa "police de sécurité quotidienne,"* édition du 5 mai; J. de Maillard & M. Zagrodzki (2021), Community Policing Initiatives in France, in de Maillard & Skogan, *Policing in France*, 294–309; M. Zagrodzki (2017), *Que fait la police? Le rôle du policier dans la société*, Paris: Editions de l'Aube.

the chiefs of the Public Security police and the commanders of the National Gendarmerie experimented with the division of responsibility between intelligence regimes, often differing radically in their decision about which intelligence regime should take the lead in analyzing and addressing collective juvenile action that ranged from retaliatory drug-related shootings in Marseille, open-air drug markets and fights between soccer fan clubs in St. Etienne, loitering in Nantes, harassment of local merchants in Cenon, assaults in Vitry-le-Francois, and fights between gangs and urban riots in the north of Paris.

In France, national legal reforms that increased the security role of mayors and increased the powers of local security partnerships reinforced a strategic decentralization and fragmentation in the approaches French law enforcement took to managing collective action, disorder, or crime involving young people. This administrative decentralization was itself a remarkable managerial concession to local variation in what otherwise remains one of the most centralized legal and policing systems in the world.

In the United States, with its focus on gangs, experimentation and change took the form of shifts between intelligence regimes rather than the fragmentation of a dominant approach. In Chicago, managerial thinking about the failures of past strategies drove a radical shift from the criminal intelligence regime and its racketeering prosecutions of gangs, to a public safety paradigm built largely on efforts to predict and prevent retaliatory shootings. During interviews in the fall of 2009, supervisors and analysts of the CPD Intelligence Unit reported that this shift had been due to the fragmentation of gangs in the wake of federal prosecutions that had jailed the leadership of Chicago largest gangs. During an interview with a supervisor of the Illinois Fusion Center, in 2015, the supervisor echoed these views, reporting that his review of changes over time in gang conflicts had led him and the CPD to conclude that rising gang shootings could be linked to the power vacuum created by the disappearance of the gangs' command hierarchy, which he believed had caused existing gangs to break into smaller units battling each other for turf. He also concluded, based on his ongoing analysis of periodic flare-ups of gang-related shootings, that the increase could be linked to shifts in federal anti-gang initiatives over time. "There was a lot of 'weed and seed' money, federal money to fight local street crime [from 1989–1999], until the money [for that] went down, [then] there was less money from the federal government. And those are the defendants that are just now getting out of jail. And they are trying to eliminate the newer competition." His analysts had linked the release of "weed and seed" defendants with a number of simultaneous trends that increased the fragmentation of drug-trafficking organization, pitting ever growing numbers of dealers from emerging organizations and emerging markets against older criminals seeking to reclaim their territory and their share of the drug trade.[221]

If Chicago switched from viewing gang crime entirely through the lens of the criminal law (and the RICO statute in particular) to viewing it almost entirely through the lens of public safety, Aurora's chief instead devised a three-pronged strategy that relied on criminal intelligence to prosecute the top tier of gang members while relying on partnership intelligence to hive off peripheral members. Aurora also developed order maintenance intelligence to identify and take action against locations that had become the focus of gang activity, relying more on the enforcement of housing ordinances than on criminal prosecutions to shut down "troubled housing" that generated graffiti, frequent complaints, and an unusual number of calls for service.[222]

In both Nantes and Aurora, by contrast, managerial decisions by municipalities and police leadership led the cities to activate local security partnerships as problem-solving intelligence regimes. Though the impetus for experimentation in Nantes came in the first instance from the municipality, partnerships in both cities gave a prominent role to civic organizations in deliberating about neighborhood-specific concerns about collective activities by juveniles and in trying out new strategies to redirect these activities based on place-specific analyses of what was driving the problem behaviors.[223]

6 Tensions between Intelligence Regimes

Our research suggests that distinct intelligence regimes conflict when one of them is asked to mimic or emulate the intelligence techniques of a distinct regime, as when order maintenance personnel are asked to act as crime scene investigators when carrying out their duties as first responders; this could interfere with frontline officers' ability to respond to emergencies in real time. One study found that patrol officers who were asked to respond to criminal intelligence like investigators

---

[221] "Cartels are being squashed. And [there's an] increase in competition in destination cities. And the offenders moved and franchised. They went to communities and delivered low cost heroin or Mexican meth faster and [delivered] cheaper or high-grade weed, some of which was not previously available. [This] destabilizes local criminal networks." The power vacuum left by successful prosecutions of gang leaders created opportunities for outsiders as well as younger, smaller remnants of the old gangs, resulting in chaos and violent competition among those left to contend for the spoils. Interview with supervisor of an Illinois fusion center, Fall 2015.

[222] Interviews with the Aurora PD's chief, lieutenants, C.O.P. officers, and municipal code enforcement officials, Fall 2009 through Summer 2010.

[223] Interviews with municipal police supervisors, police liaison officers, and municipal security officer, Nantes, Spring 2014; interviews with Aurora Cares director and directors of Aurora civic organizations, Summer 2010.

"got out of their car more, engaged citizens more, and focused on 'intelligence gathering' [to solve crimes] .... Ironically, this type of community investigation slowed responses to traditional calls for service, leading to complaints that police were unresponsive in emergencies. Further the investigatory tips generated about the targeted area were handed over to detectives without contextual information or active cases, burdening already overloaded detectives."[224]

Differences between intelligence regimes led to tensions in St. Etienne. Detective units in St. Etienne who wanted to build cases against drug wholesalers and to dismantle the command hierarchy of criminal networks were dismissive of a local community policing liaison who wanted them to build cases against retail drug vendors who were blocking access to local housing projects and intimidating residents. A new law made it possible to charge youth gangs with blocking access to common areas; but these were minor cases that rarely carried prison time, were almost always shelved by prosecutors, and almost never yielded seizures of significant drug quantities. For this reason, the chief of the detective unit (called the Surete) was unwilling to let his officers assist with the investigation of local drug dealers.[225] Yet, within the partnership paradigm, such sweeps made sense. Weisburd and Braga note that "[s]ituational strategies that modify the underlying conditions, situations, and dynamics that cause crime to cluster at specific places can be viewed as 'harm-reduction' strategies and generate positive community perceptions."[226]

Borrowing detectives from the drug unit without the chief's knowledge, the partnership liaison was able to conduct raids that interrupted local retail operations sufficiently to convince dealers to move their operations outdoors, to nearby areas that were farther removed from the housing projects, providing some relief to local residents and providing the police liaison with some credibility in the eyes of residents whose cooperation he was trying to win.

From the perspective of the chief of detectives, however, not only did the raid not result in significant prison time for any of the dealers whom the police had arrested; as a lower-echelon officer who lacked officers of his own under his command, the liaison officer (a captain) had gone outside the chain of command to poach the chief's detectives. As a result, the captain faced severe criticism from his command hierarchy after the chief of detectives complained. The liaison officer's effort to shut down open-air drug markets and to improve

---

[224] A. G. Ferguson (2017), *The Rise of Big Data Policing: Surveillance, Race, and the Future of Law Enforcement*, New York: New York University Press, 79.

[225] Interviews with partnership liaison, chief of detectives, intelligence analysts for the Sousdirection de l'Information Generale (SDIG) (formerly Renseignements Generaux), and police supervisors, St. Etienne, Spring through Fall 2013.

[226] Weisburd & Braga, *Police Innovation*, 215.

access to public housing would have aligned much better with the goals of the order maintenance regime, with its focus on reducing neighborhood nuisances than it did with the criminal intelligence regime, with its focus on building important criminal cases against high-level dealers. But the liaison was not given access to ground-level officers to carry out the raids, as patrol officers and first responders were busy ferrying prisoners to court, patrolling homes whose owners were out of town, monitoring traffic, and responding to calls for service.[227]

The police liaison officer did eventually succeed in building a working relationship with officers from St. Etienne's intelligence unit, whose surveillance reports the chief of detectives ignored because he viewed them as useless from an evidentiary perspective. The intelligence unit regularly conducted investigations of the underground economy, including drug dealing, as part of their public safety responsibility for predicting future unrest, including riots, gang violence, and turf battles between drug dealers that might threaten the long-term stability of a neighborhood and result in threats to the authority of the state (and, specifically, the development of so-called "no go zones" for the police).[228] St. Etienne's Director of Public Security had asked intelligence analysts to support the detective unit's criminal investigations of the drug trade, through surveillance of open-air drug markets.[229] Yet the public safety regime was very much at odds with the needs and expectations of the criminal intelligence regime. The surveillance reports the intelligence agents generated had no evidentiary value because intelligence analysts were not considered judicial officers (detectives). Criminal investigators could not have used the intelligence unit's reports without repeating the surveillances with designated judicial officers, to turn them into formal reports that could be included in a criminal case file (in a process known as "judicializing" an intelligence report). And while the intelligence unit's surveillance targeted largely those dealers who were the most disruptive locally, or whom they hoped to recruit as informants about unrelated matters, such as religious radicalization, these targets were often not important enough dealers in the eyes of detectives seeking to build cases against leaders of criminal organizations. That surveillance

---

[227] Interviews with partnership liaison, chief of detectives, criminal investigators, general staff, and intelligence supervisors and analysts for the SDIG (Sousdirection de l'Information Generale, formerly Renseignements Generaux, later renamed Renseignements Territoriaux), St. Etienne, Spring through Fall 2013.

[228] At the time of the interviews, the intelligence unit (formerly the Renseignements Generaux) was known as the Sousdirection de l'Information Generale (SDIG) – a slap in the face that downgraded them from an "intelligence" agency to an "information" agency before reacquiring the word "intelligence" in their title when they were renamed the Renseignements Territoriaux.

[229] Interviews with general staff of St. Etienne's Public Security police and supervisors and agents of the SDIG, Spring 2013.

reports were largely ignored by the detective unit was a source of great frustration among intelligence agents who viewed themselves as having been sidelined from their public safety assignment for largely unproductive tasks.[230]

Without access to anything like the special operations unit that Aurora's community oriented policing officers used to make undercover drug buys at places of concern to local residents, the St. Etienne partnership liaison worked closely with the frustrated intelligence agents, who helped with surveillance of street corner dealers who were blocking entrances to public housing.[231] Intelligence agents also helped the security liaison to identify local residents who were willing to file formal complaints about noise, vandalism, and assault.

The partnership liaison used the surveillances and the complaints to appeal for help to the prosecutor assigned to the local security partnership. With written complaints in place, the prosecutor was willing to charge juveniles with "abusive occupation" of common areas, to satisfy partnership demands. Though the charges were eventually dismissed, leading the chief of detectives to condemn the entire operation as a waste of time (because it did not result in jail time for the juveniles), the liaison's partners viewed the raids as successful because the arrests forced the juveniles to move and to conduct their retail operations more discreetly, to avoid disruption by the police.[232]

The police liaison benefited from this alliance by being winning the trust of residents and becoming better able to engage them and other institutional actors in discussions about situational crime prevention and how to revive recreational spaces in the neighborhood. He was able to do this in part because he found common ground with intelligence agents, who shared his interest in removing incendiary materials and changing certain physical characteristics of the neighborhood that might be contributing to car burnings and other forms of disorder that were treated as weak signals of impending riots. None of these objectives entered into the calculus of the drug unit or the chief of detectives.[233]

The intelligence unit in turn benefited from contacts with residents to recruit informants. Joining forces with the partnership liaison allowed public safety analysts of the SDIG analysts to update their long-term longitudinal data about street dealers and to investigate their overlap with local, more informal street gangs. This allowed the analysts to supply the prefect with intelligence about medium and long-term trends in high-crime neighborhoods; and the intelligence was useful to the prefect insofar as it could help him make policy

---

[230] Interviews with supervisors and analysts of the SDIG, St. Etienne, Spring 2013.

[231] Interviews with partnership liaison and supervisors and analysts of SDIG.

[232] Interviews with partnership liaison, city officials, police supervisors, and chief of detectives, St. Etienne, Spring through Summer 2013.

[233] *Ibid.*

decisions about whether to address the collective activities of young people as problems of unemployment, gangs, shifting drug turf, or signs of incipient riots. In particular, the joint surveillances allowed the intelligence chief to advise the prefect that the group could not "yet" be considered a street gang, despite their illegal activities, but that the analysts were seeking to detect any self-conscious gang affiliation (such as the display of overt gang-related graffiti) should things change.[234]

Management's failure to take account of the difference between distinct intelligence regimes resulted in these failures of coordination and undermined the operation of each regime. Gathering evidence for criminal prosecution is not the strong suit of intelligence analysts. And for the judicial police, the intelligence agents' surveillance reports about drug dealing were simply an added claim on scarce resources that were already committed to wiretaps and surveillance targeting priority suspects. Management had made no effort to align the priority targets of different regimes, resulting in conflicts between regimes that targeted high-ranking dealers (criminal intelligence); those that targeted street-level dealers who generated the most complaints (partnership intelligence); and those that could provide the most valuable intelligence about riots, gangs, or religious radicalization (the preserve of public safety intelligence). By feeding the intelligence unit's surveillance reports into the criminal intelligence regime, police leadership effectively deflected the intelligence unit's monitoring of the underground economy from those tasks for which it had been designed to others for which it was unsuited.

In the Paris prefecture, where the intelligence unit was also tasked with assisting the judicial police in conducting narcotics investigations, this tension was alleviated by the creation of joint surveillance teams, in which intelligence agents were matched with judicial officers who had arrest powers and whose reports would have evidentiary value.[235] Conducting surveillance jointly also gave the intelligence agents and the judicial police a stake in the resulting cases and an opportunity to negotiate about target selection, to ensure that the surveillance targeted at least some persons of interest to intelligence agents as well as criminal investigators.

Chicago encountered similar problems when it when it reduced its attentiveness to neighborhood concerns as relayed by district commanders and community policing officers who took part in beat meetings, thereby weakening the partnership intelligence regime in favor of a public safety approach that emphasized saturation tactics and shifted resources quickly between neighborhoods,

---

[234] Interviews with partnership liaison and analysts and supervisors of SDIG, Spring 2013.

[235] Interviews with supervisors of Renseignements Generaux, Paris Prefecture, Spring 2008.

depending on where public safety analysts predicted retaliatory violence. District commanders (who functioned as partnership liaisons) were told to supply public safety analysts with intelligence, but were given few operational resources to satisfy their local partners' request for intervention.[236] Community policing officers were no longer available to follow up on residents' complaints, because community policing officers had to answer calls for service (much as the order maintenance personnel in St. Etienne had to do), which reduced their time for proactive investigation of troubled housing, gang hangouts, shifting locations of open-air drug markets, and the quality of life concerns raised at their neighborhood beat meetings.

Effectively, community policing officers were mainly used to fulfill the reactive responsibilities of the order maintenance regime, with little time left over to conduct proactive knowledge work for the partnership regime. District commanders, who were supposed to serve as key liaisons,[237] were left with little operational capacity to collect or act on information about local community concerns, and they had less recourse to municipal resources as well, after the troubled housing task force reduced its follow-up on community complaints. In a mismatch of performance measures across distinct intelligence regimes, district commanders came to be judged by their ability to supply public safety analysts with intelligence about ongoing gang conflicts, rather than their success in addressing the concerns of residents and stakeholders in local security partnerships. Yet without strong relationships with local communities, and without being able to draw on proactive investigative work by community policing officers or the troubled housing task force, district commanders would have little intelligence to share with public safety analysts. The introduction of a highly centralized system of public safety policing thus came at the expense of what had been a finely tuned and decentralized system of community policing[238] in which district commanders could leverage their contacts with municipal services, like streets and sanitation or the troubled housing unit, on behalf of local residents.

Coordination of distinct intelligence regimes worked much better in Bordeaux than in St. Etienne, though both cities asked the Renseignements Territoriaux (RT) and its unit on the underground economy to assist in the investigation of drug trafficking organizations. Instead of being asked to perform surveillances that would have to be duplicated by detectives and that

---

[236] Interviews with district commanders, district analysts, and community policing officers, Chicago Police Department, Fall 2009.

[237] W. G. Skogan (1999), *Community Policing, Chicago Style*, Oxford: Oxford University Press, 92–96.

[238] *Ibid.*

lacked all evidentiary value, the RT in Bordeaux assisted at different points in the investigative time line, using their own distinct skills and administrative resources, which minimized conflict with the criminal intelligence regime. Unlike judicial police officers, the RT can conduct so-called "administrative wiretaps" before the initiation of a formal criminal investigation, to identify promising targets and their phone lines. Administrative wiretaps are subject to somewhat less stringent approval procedures (though they must still be approved in advance by a specialized commission) and do not presuppose the existence of an ongoing criminal investigation. They are often used to differentiate key players from lower level players in a criminal organization and of identifying the most important phone lines to be tapped through formal judicial wiretaps. By conducting administrative wiretaps before a criminal investigation was formally initiated, and with their own personnel, the RT could help criminal investigators to select targets and to craft the focus of future criminal investigations while sparing criminal investigators much advance legwork. In addition, the RT intervened in the final stages of a criminal investigation, using their greater access to administrative records to identify assets for seizure and forfeiture.[239]

Where coordination was relatively seamless, accordingly, different units and disparate intelligence regimes did not simply replicate the same tasks but redefined what they needed to do in ways that played to their respective skill sets, tools, and analytical frameworks. Aware that intelligence units are skilled at investigating the larger sociopolitical, demographic and economic context within which gangs or drug-trafficking networks operate, the director of the Public Security Police for the department and other members of his managerial intelligence staff targeted the underground economy in such a way that the Surete, or detective division, conducted surveillance, while the intelligence unit (the Renseignements Territoriaux, responsible for public safety intelligence) used background information they had assembled about social hierarchies in the neighborhood along with administrative wiretaps to identify promising targets along with the most active telephone lines to tap for usable evidence. With access to financial data, tax records, and social service rolls in all administrative branches of government, the intelligence service could investigate assets and intervene with seizures and forfeiture actions at the close of the criminal case and identify concomitant forms of tax fraud, which specialized task forces of criminal investigators from the groupements interregionaux (regional investigative task forces) could pursue further. In this way, the intelligence unit

---

[239] Interviews with partnership liaisons, criminal investigators, general staff, commanders and captains of street-level units, and supervisors and analysts of Renseignements Territoriaux, Bordeaux and suburb of Cenon, Winter and Spring 2014.

supported criminal investigators at the beginning and the end of their investigations, while staying within its own civil-administrative role and without interfering with the criminal surveillance work that made up the bulk of the detectives' metier.[240]

In Aurora, too, police leadership found a way to rely on distinct intelligence regimes in ways that played to their strengths and produced synergies instead of tensions. Aurora's police chief used a three-pronged strategy to fight gangs, delegating experienced detectives to the federal task force, allowing criminal intelligence to leverage federal resources in an effort to build cases against the leadership of major gangs simultaneously, so neither of the two main gangs could profit by the dismantling of its rival.

But the chief also launched parallel initiatives to operate largely independently of the task force, drawing on partnership and order maintenance intelligence to identify and address gang-related hot spots in different neighborhoods. The parallel initiatives relied heavily on a very decentralized system of partnership intelligence that drew on consultation in beat meetings between residents and community oriented policing officers, who followed up by proactively investigating problems and areas of concern to local residents and by helping to connect local residents with city and community resources for enforcement of new landlord–tenant ordinances. Beat meetings were used to discuss new community-wide strategies to disrupt gang recruitment and walk-throughs helped identify problem areas for follow-up by community policing officers and for further analysis by a lieutenant. The lieutenant in turn put the reports of different C.O.P. officers together to conduct a problem-oriented analysis that sought to understand the causes behind problems at particular locations, and to identify sector-wide links to gang activity.[241]

The lieutenant was in charge of order maintenance units and could make these available to implement a strategy aimed at problems and concerns identified in partnership meetings, as C.O.P. officers – partnership liaisons who also served as bridges to the order maintenance regime – were given access to their own operational resources, as special operations officers who were part of the order maintenance infrastructure worked closely with C.O.P. officers to do undercover buys and surveillance at hot spots identified by C.O.P. officers. Through their partnership contacts, the C.O.P. officers also had the city

---

[240] *Ibid.*

[241] Interviews with the Aurora PD's chief, commanders, detectives who participated in federal task force on gangs, community oriented policing officers, lieutenants, special operations officers, municipal code enforcement officials, community activists, directors of recreational centers, founder of Aurora Cares, along with participation in beat meetings and community walk-alongs, Fall 2009 through Summer 2010.

connections to mobilize ordinance enforcement, anti-graffiti details, and to experiment with other tactics when these seemed more promising. Order maintenance intelligence about ongoing emergencies and calls for service also became a resource rather than a constraint on C.O.P. officers, as they could choose to respond to a call for service from a place they had already identified as a problem location, but were not obligated to interrupt their proactive work to respond to calls for service that were of little informational value to them.

The chief's strategy was premised on closely coordinating partnership and order maintenance intelligence, while the criminal intelligence regime operated largely independently of the other regimes. Each of these prongs of the chief's strategy targeted different manifestations of the gang problem using the distinct intelligence traditions and resources of their respective regimes. Community oriented policing officers were judged by qualitative criteria focused on their success in building a close rapport with their local communities. They were also judged by how well they used proactive methods to identify and analyze a diverse array of problems in their neighborhood; and by their willingness to try out new enforcement tactics. Lieutenants, too, were judged more by their ability to give convincing and well-researched analyses of the problems in their sector, rather than by monthly fluctuations in crime rates, on the understanding that crime rates were influenced by the work amalgam of the different intelligence regimes, not the work of any individual regime.

Thus cities that coordinated distinct intelligence regimes more successfully did not simply dismantle one to build up the others, or to do the work of another regime less well. Places like Bordeaux and Aurora used each regime to do what it did best – not to mimic the methods or be evaluated by the performance measures peculiar to a different regime. The managerial intelligence regime used its access to longitudinal data about changes over time in crime and police performance to select a strategy that prioritized one or more intelligence regimes. The strategy also included decisions about whether and how to coordinate the work of distinct intelligence regimes. When intelligence regimes were coordinated, this was done in ways that drew on the respective strengths of each.

Depending on how they are coordinated, then, distinct intelligence regimes can cooperate with each other, work at cross purposes, compete, or work entirely independently of each other. Managing their coexistence should be one of the main tasks of the managerial intelligence regime. Our typology suggests that the problems a city has encountered in implementing its chosen strategy can sometimes be traced to tensions between distinct regimes who have been asked to work together on a given problem. Cross-national as well as subnational comparisons can illuminate the factors that create synergy or conflict between intelligence regimes that are called upon to cooperate and to coordinate their interventions. By assigning different intelligence regimes to different temporal phases of the same investigation, for example, the command hierarchy can ask each regime to do what it does best, without creating redundancies and blockages of the sort that occurred when public safety was asked to support the criminal intelligence unit's surveillance of open-air drug markets.

7 What Does Our Typology Have to Say about Intelligence-Led Policing?

Emerging in the 1990s in the UK, Australia, and the US, intelligence-led policing is a "business model" that seeks to improve the ways in which law enforcement agencies design strategy to mitigate public safety concerns and to give police management "a better capacity to identify, understand and respond to a broad range of crime and order issues."[242] Intelligence-led policing is meant to assist the police in making more effective use of limited resources, by proactively targeting "particular people, locations and behaviors in a highly systematic way, often in partnership with other agencies." The aim was to "seek 'solutions' which eradicate or reduce the problem or the activity, not merely the arrest or conviction of a few individuals."[243]

Intelligence-led policing also holds the promise of going beyond a role of assisting criminal investigations, as part of a concerted effort to improve the way the police address quality of life issues, antisocial behavior, the improved handling of calls for service, and public safety concerns about terrorism.[244] Intelligence-led policing suggests that police think about organized crime and terrorism "in terms of proactive enforcement, opportunity reduction, disruption and prevention."[245] This new "business model" for policing became institutionalized in the US when IACP and the DOJ's Office of Community Oriented

---

[242] J. W. E. Sheptycki & J. H. Ratcliffe (2009), Setting the Strategic Agenda, in J. H. Ratcliffe, ed., *Strategic Thinking in Criminal Intelligence*, 2nd ed., Sydney: The Federation Press, 248–268; M. Innes & J. W. E. Sheptycki (2004), From Detection to Disruption: Intelligence and the Changing Logic of Police Crime Control in the United Kingdom, *International Criminal Justice Review* 14:1–24. Sheptycki defines proactive police as the deployment of police resources "on the basis of crime analysis (e.g. the geo-temporal crime pattern analysis) with the intention of affecting some future situation." Sheptycki, The Police Intelligence Division of Labor.

[243] M. Maguire (2000), Policing by Risk and Targets: Some Dimensions and Implications of Intelligence Led Crime Control, *Policing and Society* 9(4):315–336, 333.

[244] S. Christopher & N. Cope (2009), A Practitioner's Perspective of UK Strategic Intelligence, in Ratcliffe, *Strategic Thinking*, 235–247, 237.

[245] Sheptycki, The Police Intelligence Division of Labor; Innes & Sheptycki, From Detection to Disruption; J. McCulloch & D. Wilson (2016), *Pre-crime: Pre-emption, Precaution and the Future*, London: Routledge.

Policing Services (COPS) and Bureau of Justice Assistance enacted intelligence-led policing guidelines for local police.

Though intelligence-led policing originated in English-speaking countries, French policing, too, has becoming more intelligence-led, as the French National Police has moved SIRASCO, its criminal intelligence unit closer to its investigative units,[246] to create operational outflows for intelligence and to make it easier for intelligence analysis to influence decision-making processes, not only of investigators but of those who set investigative priorities and allocate resources to criminal investigations. As further discussed below, France has emulated the Compstat system and has increased its reliance on new surveillance technologies, data mining, and algorithms in an effort to make a more efficient use of its law enforcement resources and its domestic intelligence agencies. France has sought to integrate local security partnerships into its intelligence-led strategy, as such partnerships became the eyes and ears of the police after the abolition of community policing in 2003. What remains a challenge in both the United States and in France is the coordination of multiple intelligence regimes by the command hierarchy.

For all its promise, ILP depends on law enforcement agencies' "ability to collect, analyze, disseminate, and integrate intelligence into the operations of the organization."[247] This presupposes a good match with intelligence regimes whose time horizons, preferred collection methods, established analytical practices, and operational routines fit well with what the regime will be asked to do. Peter Manning notes that police tend to use intelligence tools in ways that match their working philosophy and their familiar operational routines.[248] "The reaches of technology are limited by the ecology of the organization," he contends, and uptake will depend on how close informational tools are "to the routine pathways and practices of officers."[249] If patrol officers, whose responsibilities are largely reactive, have little use for sophisticated tools like link analysis, organized crime divisions or gang unit analysts whose investigative tactics are much more proactive embrace such tools eagerly, as these technologies fit with their tasks, outlook, time horizons – and with the ecology of actors, such as gang investigators, prosecutors, financial analysts, moles, undercover agents, and task force partners with whom they cooperate. Not only must managerial decision-makers and advisers "know 'what works' in policing and crime reduction,"[250] they must

---

[246] Interview with intelligence supervisor, French National Police, Fall 2021.

[247] Carter, *Intelligence-Led Policing*, 23.

[248] P. K. Manning (2008), *The Technology of Policing: Crime Mapping, Information Technology, and the Rationality of Crime Control*, New York: New York University Press.

[249] Manning, Technology, Law, and Policing, 303.

[250] J. H. Ratcliffe (2009), The Structure of Strategic Thinking, in Ratcliffe, *Strategic Thinking*, 1–10, 9.

also understand which intelligence regime is best suited to which types of strategies.

Accordingly, intelligence-led approaches need to fit the intelligence regime in which they will be embedded. The case method and the focus on prolific offenders, for example, is best matched with criminal intelligence, while efforts to abate risks more efficiently are best assigned to the public safety regime. When Carter describes Ratcliffe's 2008 model of intelligence-led policing as one that uses crime analysis and a focus on prolific offenders to solve cases and bring down crime, he implicitly assigns Ratcliffe's version of ILP to the criminal intelligence and order maintenance regimes. Recent scholarly suggestions that the police should couple intelligence-led policing with problem-solving approaches[251] and external partnerships suggest the applicability of proactive, intelligence-led approaches to other realms of police work than criminal investigations.

Carter implicitly matches his own version of intelligence-led policing with the public safety and partnership approaches when he describes his model as more focused on threats and suspicious behaviors and more apt than Ratcliffe's to draw on "the communities of multiple jurisdictions," the private sector, and public health institutions.[252] Accordingly, Carter takes the view that police productivity should be measured by "threats mitigated or prevented or strategies priorities identified ... as a result of analysis reports,"[253] replacing or at least supplementing a focus on crime with a focus on threats. Ratcliffe himself eventually came to take a more ecumenical view of the aims of intelligence-led policing, when he expanded the range of objectives that intelligence-led policing can help the police to maximize beyond crime reduction to harm reduction.[254] Harms can encompass quality of life concerns other than crime and can be reduced through means other than the case method, making ILP applicable to intelligence regimes other than the criminal intelligence paradigm.

But that is more easily said than done, and we use our typology of intelligence regimes to suggest what harm reduction might mean outside of the criminal intelligence paradigm. The difficulty of thinking about harms in different terms – of "escaping" from the criminal intelligence paradigm – is suggested by Ratcliffe's discussion of a controlled experiment known as the

---

[251] M. Maguire & T. John (2006), Intelligence Led Policing, Managerialism and Community Engagement: Competing Priorities and the Role of the National Intelligence Model in the UK, *Policing and Society* 16(1):67–85; D. Oakensen, R. Mockford, & C. Pascoe (2002), Does There Have to be Blood on the Carpet? Integrating Partnership, Problem-Solving and the National Intelligence Model in Strategic and Tactical Police Decision-Making Processes, *Police Research and Management* 5(4):51–62.

[252] Carter, *Intelligence-Led Policing*, 25.   [253] *Ibid.*, 58.

[254] Ratcliffe, *Intelligence-Led Policing*, 2nd ed.

"Swiss Experiment." The experiment "showed that acquisitive crime by heroin users declined substantially under a prescription regime. Other criteria of harm related to the social well-being of drug takers, such as being able to maintain employment and steady social relationships, and their general physical and psychological health ... also indicated a positive influence attributable to the prescription regime," suggesting the need for "strategies that require outcome measures that are different from those that typically shape the criminal intelligence process. Unlike traditional approaches to controlling organized crime, strategic harm-based approaches cannot be assessed on the basis of purely law enforcement outcomes."[255] Harm reduction therefore requires input from other intelligence paradigms.

Other intelligence regimes might remedy the blind spots of a harm-reduction approach embedded within a criminal intelligence paradigm. Natasha Tusikov notes, for example, that a criminal intelligence unit's risk assessments of street gangs often focuses on profit-driven activities of gangs, even though "[s]treet gangs ... are involved in a variety of activities without direct financial gain, such as graffiti, to promote and protect gang identity and territory." One reason for this is that "criminal intelligence has adopted ... a market-based perspective," which allows analysts to apply "models of legitimate businesses and the legitimate market ... to criminal markets."[256] The criminal intelligence regime's embrace of market models of crime leads its analysts to ignore the social cost of less profit-driven activities such as vandalism and conflict over turf. Vandalism and graffiti may be of greater concern to order maintenance and partnership intelligence, however, which could deal with these social costs by experimenting with ways of reclaiming public spaces for communal purposes. Partnership regimes are also alert to fear of crime and distrust of public authorities as harms in their own right, while the order maintenance intelligence focuses more on harms that take the form of demands for emergency services (for which the Aurora Police Department actually sought restitution from landlords of troubled housing that generated excessive emergency calls for gang-related violence). Public safety analysts, in turn, may focus more on gang-related violence than on profit-driven crime, as uncontrolled violence may cause political problems for city and police leadership.

We suggest that the pursuit of harm reduction requires practitioners of ILP to decide which intelligence regime is most suited to a particular problem. And this in turn may depend on the scale of the problem. In Goldstein's view,

---

[255] J. W. E. Sheptycki & J. H. Ratcliffe (2004), Setting the Strategic Agenda, in J. H. Ratcliffe, ed., *Strategic Thinking in Criminal Intelligence*, Sydney: The Federation Press, 194–216, 206.

[256] N. Tusikov & R.C. Fahlman (2009), Threat and Risk Assessments, in Ratcliffe, *Strategic Thinking in Criminal Intelligence*, 147–164.

"problems ought to be explored as close to the operating level as possible . . . The broader the inquiry, the more it is removed from the context in which the problem exists, the more it appears to be drained of much of the richness and creativity reflected in localized inquiries."[257] Accordingly, Goldstein favors the partnership model, which requires "dialogue between the police and the community," or "door-to-door surveys," and that police "extend themselves in order to learn about the concerns of the community."[258] However, citywide problems that require resources to be shifted quickly across considerable geographical areas on the basis of predictive algorithms may be better addressed through public safety policing, with its reliance on rapid deployment teams that can range quickly over a broad area and its focus on predicting and abating future violence that ranges widely across neighborhoods. Viewing harm reduction through the lenses of different intelligence regimes is one way of contributing to "a growing literature on harm reduction and regulatory strategies that is only slowly being integrated with the literature on intelligence led policing."[259]

Understanding the differences between intelligence regimes also suggests some ways of calling into question the appropriateness of targeting criteria that intelligence-led policing sometimes takes for granted. One of these is resiliency of a criminal organization. The ways in which criminal organizations respond to the arrest of ringleaders could have conflicting implications, depending on the focus of the intelligence regime that assesses the harms of organized crime. Criminal intelligence regimes view highly resilient criminal organizations as much more serious threats than ones that can be easily crushed by incapacitating it leadership, and intelligence-led policing often treats resilient organizations as priority targets. But from the public safety perspective, highly resilient organizations may be more successful at keeping out competitors and therefore less violent. Taking down a particularly large and powerful criminal organization can lead to power struggles among successors and may lead to the kind of fragmentation into smaller, more violent street gangs whose emergence prompted Chicago's switch to a public safety framework.

However, to question basic assumptions about resiliency as a metric of an organization's threat potential, one has to stand outside of the criminal intelligence framework. Our typology suggests what it would mean to adopt an alternative framework. Threat assessments embedded in a managerial framework, for example, are less likely to be captured by metrics like resiliency that ignore the unintended effects of targeting criminal organizations on the basis of their resiliency; within the managerial framework, analysts may be more willing

---

[257] Goldstein, *Problem-Oriented Policing*, 69–70.   [258] *Ibid.*, 71.
[259] Sheptycki & Ratcliffe (2004), Setting the Strategic Agenda, 207.

to question the primacy of criminal intelligence as the preferred approach to a crime problem and may be more open to working with residents, religious leaders, schools, and other nonpolice actors in trying out approaches like Pulling Levers in Boston. But the opportunity costs of assigning threat and risk assessments to analysts embedded within detective units only become visible when one recognizes the difference between criminal intelligence and managerial intelligence, as the latter takes account of the public safety effects of targeting resilient organizations along with the order maintenance effects (such as the destabilizing impact on a neighborhood), among other unintended consequences that lie beyond the purview of the criminal intelligence regime.

Though informed by a threat assessment's ranking of harms, the managerial intelligence regime's decisions about which regime's approach to select as the dominant approach and how to coordinate it with that of other regimes is likely to be a deeply political and pragmatic one that may be driven, in part, by considerations about which intelligence regime has tried and failed to handle a particular problem; which has the most unused capacity; which units are deemed the most professional and reliable; which have recently been involved in a scandal; and which security problems may cost political leaders the next election. Accordingly, threat and risk assessments performed for the managerial regime may need to go beyond rankings of threats to inform the command hierarchy of which intelligence regime may be the most appropriate to tackle the diverse harms analysts have identified.

The managerial intelligence perspective becomes particularly important when threat and risk analysis pulls back the lens to expose links between licit and illicit sectors of society. The managerial regime will have an important role in determining which intelligence regime will be best able to disrupt those links. In Marseille, for example, the Unite de Prevention Urbaine, which maintained links to neighborhood recreational centers and nurtured partnerships with civil society, was able to warn the prefect about associations that had been taken over by narcotics dealers. Intelligence about relationships between organized crime and licit sectors might also draw on order maintenance intelligence about neighborhood establishments that were paying "street tax" to organized crime, cooperating with extremist organizations, or generating unusual numbers of calls for service due to illicit activities.[260] The public safety regime in St. Etienne was, in turn, well positioned to learn about simmering social conflicts between construction companies and local youth groups seeking to have their members hired as work crews.[261] And sometimes managerial

---

[260] Interview with UPU supervisor, Summer 2015.

[261] Interviews with social worker and intelligence analysts (SDIG), St. Etienne, Spring 2013.

intelligence can call for more fundamental structural changes to licit institutions, to protect them from infiltration by illicit sectors, as when a city randomizes the assignment of cases to judges to reduce opportunities for corruption, or, more dramatically, when the federal government took over the Teamsters to reduce the grip of organized crime on the union.

In the US, our research identifies the important role of state fusion centers in adapting ILP to the characteristics of distinct intelligence regimes. For example, fusion centers supply police leadership with managerial intelligence about what works and what doesn't work, advising police, for example, that there is no crime data to suggest that gang members buy their weapon at gun shows, so that increased supervision of gun shows is unlikely to abate gang violence.[262] This kind of intelligence is useful to police leadership in deciding whether to monitor gun shows primarily from an order maintenance perspective, to keep the peace and monitor compliance with safety rules, or whether to use gun shows as a source of criminal intelligence about gangs and their weapons. A Florida fusion center developed managerial intelligence about how administrative interventions can disrupt organized crime more effectively than criminal prosecution. "If you just arrest mobsters, they'll resume crimes later," a fusion center supervisor claimed. "So we pulled in other agencies to dismantle [criminal] organizations... Business and occupation licenses [were] pulled. The department of revenue [took action] against gambling operations."[263]

The Florida Fusion Center likewise developed managerial intelligence about how the state should balance public health public health initiatives that treat problems like bath salts as public safety threats with crime-fighting initiatives like the enactment of new criminal prohibitions on the sale of bath salts.[264] Based in part on hospital notifications about the effects of the chemicals and in part on "open source materials, newspaper articles, as well as reports from police on emerging drugs, and journals" about why young people were inhaling these substances, the fusion center convinced the Florida attorney general to issue an emergency order prohibiting the sale of these substances from a public safety perspective, while attempting to determine whether organized crime had taken over the sale of bath salts, which might counsel the enactment of legislation to list the salts as controlled substances whose sale would incur criminal penalties.[265]

Fusion centers also develop intelligence-led approaches for the order maintenance regime. Based on its statistical analysis of domestic violence patterns, for example, an Illinois fusion center advised the order maintenance supervisors

---

[262] Interview with supervisor of an Illinois fusion center, Fall 2015.
[263] Interview with Supervisor of a Florida fusion center, Spring 2009.   [264] *Ibid.*
[265] Interview with supervisor of a Tallahassee fusion center, Spring 2009.

who dispatch ground-level personnel that they could reduce the incidence of domestic violence emergencies through preventive deployments of ground-level officers, to take account of the fusion center's finding that "the delivery of an order of protection and of divorce orders [are] destabilizing events" that have regularly been linked to killings of domestic partners. To reduce the incidence of emergencies arising out of the service of legal process, the fusion center suggested changing the way abusers are notified of legal orders, by "sending a minister and a police officer along with the court officers" whenever such papers are served to someone accused of domestic abuse.[266] And to improve its own handling of incoming calls for assistance from order-maintenance personnel, the Fusion Center sent analysts to the headquarters of a large airline "to figure out how you run a call center and communicate with the public."[267]

Most fusion centers focus their intelligence-led expertise on public safety matters, from national security and disaster preparedness to crowd control at sporting events, much as the Renseignements Territoriaux do in France. "We look at all major [upcoming] public events in Illinois ... and we look at what organizations are present and how many people will show up," the supervisor of an Illinois fusion center reported. If a number of the protesters seen at past events and anticipated at future events are, say, "IRA members, we can assess the impact on public safety." In planning for the NATO summit in Illinois, "we looked at who's coming, how many," though "we can't look at names unless there's a threat of a crime, like 'I will burn the city down'. We assess people who are confirmed threats or who may be a threat, and we follow anarchists and can predict violence."[268] Fusion center analysts help with planning for the event through "predictive assessments" about who might show up to disrupt an event and what they might try to do.[269] In order to learn about effective ways to abate safety threats during times of riot and public unrest, the midwestern Fusion Center also sent analysts to large multinational companies that have well-known public safety programs for protecting management from kidnappings during strikes.[270]

In the criminal intelligence realm, fusion centers develop their own intelligence-led expertise on best practices and effective strategies for using informants to dismantle criminal networks. "Right now, sources are transactional," the Illinois fusion center supervisor reported, meaning that an informant will be deployed against the particular person or group of people the informant brings to the attention of the police. Much like a supervisor of the Marseille judicial

---

[266] Interview with supervisor of an Illinois fusion center, Fall 2015.   [267] *Ibid.*   [268] *Ibid.*
[269] *Ibid.*   [270] *Ibid.*

police, who developed a program that revised the debriefing of informants, the supervisor criticized the current approach, as it leaves the targeting initiative to informants, that is, to someone who is usually a criminal and may have corrupt motivations. "I'll double the pay of an informant to fill in blanks in what we know" about an organization that the police is already targeting on its own initiative, the supervisor insisted. Instead of building occasional cases as the opportunity arises, informants will remain situated in an organization so they can regularly acquire information in a targeted way, "to pivot informants so they will be used to complete the [organizational] picture," filling the gaps in what the police already know, not in what the informant wants the police to know.[271]

And while intelligence-led policing promotes "proactive" modes of policing, our typology helps to give regime-specific content to that prescription. Proactive partnership approaches may mobilize communities to talk about why so many members of a particular age group are joining gangs and how to draw them into recreational offerings. Proactive order maintenance approaches may involve undercover drug buys at open-air drug markets, in the US, or visual surveillance, in France. Proactive criminal intelligence tactics may instead counsel gathering evidence that will allow investigators to dismantle a gang's leadership rather than making small individual drug cases against this or that member of the organization, except when that individual is someone whom the police would like to recruit as an informant. Proactive public safety initiatives in turn monitor danger signals of impending riots or escalating gang conflicts before these reach a fever pitch. For the managerial intelligence regime, being proactive may mean identifying deficits in the operational resources available to other intelligence regimes that lack the manpower to act on what they know. Translating ILP prescriptions in this way requires an understanding of the parallel existence of multiple intelligence enclaves within the police and of the distinct task environments in which they operate.

Finally, our typology has implications for a central tenet of intelligence-led policing that recommends merging redundant intelligence capabilities to improve the flow of intelligence within the police. When the New Jersey State Police wished to introduce an intelligence-led approach to the way it conducted criminal investigations of organized crime, Ratcliffe reports, police leadership found it necessary to consolidate a street gang bureau that was part of the Intelligence Division with an intelligence unit dedicated to narcotics and organized crime within the division of Investigations.[272] The reform allowed analysts from the merged units to pool their knowledge and expertise instead of

---

[271] *Ibid.*

[272] J. H. Ratcliffe (2008), State Police Investigative Structure and the Adoption of Intelligence-Led Policing, *Policing*, 31(1):109–128, 113.

competing with one another. This consolidation made sense, we suggest, because both units were part of the criminal intelligence regime.

While ILP counsels consolidating redundant intelligence capabilities, however, our differentiation among intelligence regimes suggests that there may be value in having separate intelligence capabilities across distinct intelligence regimes. The reforms to the New Jersey State Police did not have to take account of the value of having separate intelligence units for, say, patrol, dispatch, or first-responders, because state police agencies don't have a local component in the way municipal police departments do. Unlike distinct gang and drug units within the criminal intelligence regime, distinct intelligence silos *across* intelligence regimes, we contend, if they serve fundamentally different aims, perform distinct types of knowledge work across different time horizons, function within distinct task environments.

For example, a supervisor within Marseille's Renseignements Territoriaux (RT) mentioned that he would like the chief to merge his unit with the Unité de Prévention Urbaine, the Marseille mediation unit which generates a great deal of useful intelligence for the police director.[273] But the RT are part of the public safety regime, while the UPU is a mediation unit that is built on outreach and informal consultation with external stakeholders and community residents; it comes as close as any unit in France can to engaging in a form of community policing and is the one active component of an informal partnership regime that replaces the largely dormant partnership structures of Marseille. Both the RT and the UPU yield useful intelligence, including information that they funnel to the judicial police in the criminal intelligence regime, about who is likely responsible for recent narcotics-related homicides. But the RT is largely responsible for public safety intelligence and the two units thus belong to fundamentally different regimes at heart, even if they occasionally wear other hats; and a merger with the intelligence unit would take away much of the trust and legitimacy that the UPU's mediators enjoy in the *banlieues* of Marseille. The UPU uses its local contacts as a member of the partnership regime to defuse unrest in times of crisis, as it did by leading silent marches after the accidental killing of local teenagers by a police ambulance, and it serves as the eyes and ears of the managerial regime about how police approaches are perceived by local residents, making it a useful source of managerial intelligence of a sort that the RT are not able to generate.[274] Duplication is not always redundancy, when the overlapping intelligence units – both of which are concerned with riots, narcotics dealing,

---

[273] Interview with RT supervisor, Marseille, Summer 2015.

[274] Interview with UPU supervisor, Summer 2015.

and homicides – are embedded in the fundamentally different intelligence
traditions that we call regimes.

8 Conclusion

The notion of an intelligence regime is thus a new way of refracting any given
city's security policy across the spectrum of the five distinct professional
communities and interpretive frameworks that make up a city's security architecture; a new way of explaining conflict and occasional synergies among
security elites within the same city and even within the same police department;
and a new way of making cities comparable across and within national boundaries. In particular, we contend that any organization's approach to problems
such as collective offending by juveniles are defined by the peculiar constellation of intelligence regimes that play some part in addressing the problem. This
constellation is not only determined by which intelligence regime takes the lead
in solving the problem (as public safety does in Chicago). A police department's
configuration of intelligence regimes also reflects decisions about whether some
intelligence regimes are expected to play a subordinate and supportive role to
others, as Chicago's criminal intelligence regime did in in serving up a steady
stream of pretext prosecutions to assist the public safety regime, or whether
intelligence regimes function largely independently of each other, as the criminal and partnership intelligence regimes did in Aurora.

The task of configuring the respective roles of distinct intelligence regimes
explains why "intelligence bureaus [working for police leadership] are seen to
be increasingly important in the orchestration of the police intelligence div-
ision-of labor."[275] In identifying ideal-typical intelligence regimes that transcend systemic differences between the United States and France, we theorize
such a division of knowledge work within the police by suggesting how intelligence regimes within any given police organization will differ in their approach
to complex problems.

The same security problem may look very different to members of distinct
intelligence regimes within the same organization. Through the lens of the
criminal intelligence regime, gang violence generates efforts to prove past
offenses. This approach will likely involve criminal investigators and prosecutors (and, sometimes, investigative judges, in France) rather than intelligence
analysts predicting future outbreaks of violence, or rapid intervention teams
seeking to saturate at-risk neighborhoods. The political salience of "threats"
(not "crimes") unites the public safety concerns of French analysts who worry

---

[275] Sheptycki, The Police Intelligence Division of Labor.

about "urban violence" by young people with those of Chicago's analysts who seek to project and to interrupt the trajectory of ongoing gang conflicts.

For order maintenance specialists, in turn, the salient feature of collective juvenile offending is its impact not on the state but on members of the public; the solution may be the development of crime reduction initiatives (leaning heavily on problem-oriented approaches and hot spot policing, with their emphasis on the policing of problem spaces) to alleviate residents' fears and to reduce the demand for emergency services. Accordingly, collective juvenile offending may be more likely to be treated as a quality of life issue for neighbors and a threat to housing values than as a crisis that challenges the political leadership's ability to keep people safe and govern effectively. For partnership policing, collective juvenile offending is a problem that requires a combination of preventive and crime-fighting strategies, targeting locations, individuals, or groups, which can be variously identified as gangs, age groups in need of recreational spaces or residents of a particular housing complex, depending on jointly elaborated and negotiated analyses by decision-makers both inside and outside the police. And if treated as an occasion for managerial oversight and strategic choices, collective juvenile offending calls forth efforts to assess the respective effectiveness of past approaches in order to select the intelligence regime that should take the lead in tackling a given problem and to coordinate that regime with others that are asked to support it.

The security policy of any given site, then, is a function of the leadership's strategic choices about which problems to assign primarily to which regime and how to coordinate the lead regime with others that are asked to support the dominant regime's approach. Understanding the influence of the regime on problem-definition makes it possible to compare how the partnership regime's treatment of juvenile delinquency in Aurora compares with the partnership regime's approach to the problem in St. Etienne. Assimilating subnational to cross-national comparisons also makes it possible to discern similarities between the approaches that cities like Marseille and Chicago take to collective juvenile violence – similarities that bring them closer to each other than they may be to the security strategies of other cities in their own countries, in that each city has selected a public safety approach to problems of collective juvenile offending. Refracting a city's security strategy through the lenses of its distinct intelligence regime also reveals synergies or pathologies peculiar to the ways in which the system has coordinated these regimes (as the comparisons of Bordeaux and St. Etienne suggest) and can in turn suggest which types of outside expertise match best with which regimes. An algorithmic approach to predicting violence, for example, will become a significant tool in a city like Chicago which has adopted a public safety approach to collective juvenile offending, while the expertise of civic organizations working with at-risk juveniles will matter more to a place like Aurora that has emphasized partnership initiatives to slow recruitment of new gang members during the lull created by the simultaneous prosecution of two competing gangs.

Our typology captures the characteristic preoccupations of distinct intelligence regimes across both sides of the Atlantic, and our research suggests that these ideal types transcend the significant institutional differences between a highly centralized and a highly decentralized security architecture. As distinct ways of collecting, analyzing, and using information about security concerns such as gangs, intelligence regimes differ along a number of key dimensions. These dimensions include the time horizons of interest to each regime; the regimes' respective ways of carving up crime problems (into cases, threats, situations, stakeholder concerns, or calls on police resources, depending on the regime and its lens); the regimes' respective criteria of relevance and validity; and their preferred tools and associated expectations about what analysts must do to turn information into actionable intelligence. Intelligence regimes also coalesce around distinctive ecologies of actors who share and use the relevant information, and these actors' insights feed into disparate actions and routines.

Understanding the police as an amalgam of distinct intelligence regimes also helps explain why it matters to the policing of gangs or other complex phenomena whether the relevant law enforcement agency is a generalist institution or a specialist agency, as federal agencies tend to be. Generalist agencies house multiple distinct intelligence regimes, making it possible for analysts to go well beyond the public safety and criminal intelligence perspectives available to federal investigators. This multiplies not only the lenses (and time horizons) through which security problem are analyzed but also expands the range of mechanisms available to address them. Intelligence-led approaches to collective juvenile offending, we contend, are mediated by the intelligence regimes through which they are implemented, so that efforts to address a given problem will look very different across regime boundaries. Intelligence-led policing can help maximize an outcome, like undermining resilient crime groups; but to question which outcome one wishes to maximize, decision-makers must not be fully captured by the framework of any one regime but able to assess possible outcomes from the vantage point of the other four regimes, as managerial intelligence seeks to do, before selecting between them.

Accordingly, our aims are both explanatory and normative. Uptake of intelligence reform is more likely when reforms build on the knowledge work the police already perform. The notion of an intelligence regime is one way of organizing that ongoing knowledge work. Intelligence-led strategies are mediated and shaped by the intelligence regimes through which data are analyzed and funneled into an action-repertoire or range of possible interventions. Determining how to reform a police department makes it necessary to ascertain which intelligence regimes have thus far taken the lead in tackling a particular problem, like gang violence; how distinct regimes have been coordinated in their approach to a given problem; and whether this is producing conflict or synergies. Our exploration of tensions and synergies between regimes thus allows us to explain why Bordeaux has encountered so much less resistance than St. Etienne to reforms that have assigned intelligence bureaus the task of supporting the interdiction of retail drug rings. Our theory supplies the categories for subnational and cross-national comparisons of organizational strategies, revealing why Chicago and Marseille have more in common with each other's approaches to the narcotics-related violence than Marseille has with Nantes or than Chicago has with Aurora.

Thus, if intelligence-led policing can improve the functioning of each intelligence regime, it can also guide managerial intelligence in its selection of an approach from among the available regimes and in coordinating the dominant regime(s) with the others to create synergies between them (while avoiding some of the pitfalls identified above). Asking each regime to do what it does best can avoid the redundancies and blockages of the sort that occurred in St. Etienne, when public safety agents were called upon to support the criminal intelligence unit's prosecution of drug dealers. Our research thus suggests new ways in which analysts can function as vectors of intelligence-led policing, by adapting ILP to each regime's characteristic task environment, including its distinctive time horizons, ecology of actors, criteria of validity, and so forth.

We note that the five regimes are not only a constraint (e.g. on the uptake of reforms by the police), but a resource, as they identify existing capacities on which reformers can build and which a chief who understands their respective strengths and limitations can choose among and coordinate. They are a constraint because, as Weisburd and Braga note, "the adoption of innovation is determined primarily by the experiences of practitioners and often has little to do with research evidence."[276] Assigning any given initiative to the right regime, whose practitioners can call on their own experience with kindred tactics or analytical frameworks, can encourage uptake of reforms. Police already carry out diverse forms of knowledge work in their distinct intelligence regimes.[277] If "[p]olice

---

[276] D. Weisburd & A. Braga (2006), Hot Spots Policing as a Model for Police Innovation, in *Police Innovation*, 225–244, 238.

[277] Acknowledging the importance of ensuring fit between scientific research and the knowledge work already being performed by the police, Fyfe prefers the term "knowledge-based" policing to "evidence-based" policing, as the former "embraces the diversity of knowledge ('craft', 'scientific', 'professional', 'experiential') that informs police decision-making rather than privileging research evidence." N. R. Fyfe (2018), Police Research, Evidence-Based

departments are highly resistant to change and police officers often experience difficulty in implementing new programs,"[278] the prospects of any given reform initiative will depend to a great extent on the selection of a regime to take the lead in implementing the reform. How police receive outside recommendations will depend on how well data, tools, and recommended action plans fit with ongoing knowledge work in the respective intelligence regimes we identify and distinguish from each other. Understanding the characteristics of these regimes is essential to assessing the fit between recommendations and established practice, and to identifying the intelligence regime most likely to have some affinity for the tools and analytical frameworks proffered by outsiders.

But intelligence regimes are also opportunities. They permit police leadership to delegate problem-solving to the most appropriate among the discrete ecologies of actors who make up a given intelligence regime, depending on management's own assessment of which regime and thus which lens to privilege. Doing so effectively requires the command hierarchy to understand what it is that the managerial intelligence regime can do and what role confusions to avoid. For example, recentralization of police operations by the managerial regime "inhibits the problem-solving capabilities" of the police[279] and conflicts with Goldstein's recommendation that problem-solving occur at a "street level of analysis,"[280] which would be better handled by the order maintenance or partnership regimes. Managerial intelligence is a meta-regime, whose access to metadata about police performance is used more effectively to evaluate, choose between, and coordinate the other four regimes – not to take over their functions.

As an ideal-typical construct, the intelligence regime not only explains what police already do and makes diverse sites and strategies comparable. It also suggests reasons for simmering internal tensions along with means of reducing them; recasts the managerial role of the command hierarchy as one of coordinating the division of labor between the ongoing knowledge work of multiple intelligence regimes; generates insights into ways of building on what police already do and of adapting intelligence-led approaches to fit with the intelligence regime most likely to be receptive to such an approach; and it suggests that, in many places, police reform can be reconstructed as "regime change" between competing analytical frameworks within the same institution.

Policing and Police-Academic Partnerships in National Jurisdictions, in M. den Boer, *Comparative Policing from a Legal Perspective*, 407–422, 412.

[278] Braga & Weisburd, Conclusion, 339.

[279] Weisburd, Mastrofski, Willis, & Greenspan, Changing Everything, 285.

[280] Goldstein, *Problem-Oriented Policing*.

Acknowledgments

We are extremely grateful for the feedback and advice we received from Andrew Leipold, Andrea Roth, Christopher Slobogin, Fabien Jobard, Jacques de Maillard, James Sheptycki, James Q. Whitman, Jason Mazzone, Jonathan Simon, Jeremie Gauthier, Laurent Mayali, Malcolm Feeley, Ron Levi, and Richard Ross, and for the generous research support of the Agence Nationale de Recherche of France, of France's Centre National de Recherche Scientifique, which hosted Jacqueline Ross at Cachan during the 2007–2008 academic year, and of the Fulbright Association, whose grant funded the research of Jacqueline Ross in France during the 2007–2008 academic year. Many thanks to Margarita Vassileva, who skillfully administered all our research contracts and to Commissioners Eric Plaisant and Didier Rosselin of the French National Police Research Center and to Colonels Philippe Durand and Jean-Marc Jaffré, of the National Gendarmerie Research Center, who helped provide us with access to fieldwork sites in France and helped make it possible for us to use the results to train French police managers.

To my parents, Jana and Friedrich Katz
-J.R.
to Marjolaine and Charles.
- T.D.

Cambridge Elements ⁼

Criminology

Elements in the Series

Developmental Criminology and the Crime Decline
Jason L. Payne, Alexis R. Piquero

A Framework for Addressing Violence and Serious Crime
Anthony A. Braga, David M. Kennedy

Whose 'Eyes on the Street' Control Crime?: Expanding Place Management into Neighborhoods
Shannon J. Linning, John E. Eck

Confronting School Violence: A Synthesis of Six Decades of Research
Jillian J. Turanovic, Travis C. Pratt, Teresa C. Kulig, Francis T. Cullen

Testing Criminal Career Theories in British and American Longitudinal Studies
John F. MacLeod, David P. Farrington

Legitimacy-Based Policing and the Promotion of Community Vitality
Tom Tyler, Caroline Nobo

Making Sense of Youth Crime: A Comparison of Police Intelligence in the United States and France
Jacqueline E. Ross, Thierry Delpeuch

A full series listing is available at: www.cambridge.org/ECRM

Printed in the United States
by Baker & Taylor Publisher Services